NO JUSTICE

By
Angelica Soul

ISBN-13: 978-1544242231

ISBN-10: 1544242239

Design & formatting by Socciones Editoria Digitale
www.kindle-publishing-service.co.uk

This book is dedicated to my mum who sadly passed in 2013. I would also like to thank my friend Carol who gave me the support and encouragement to write this book.

Thank you, Mum and Carol.

Some of the names in this book have been changed in order to preserve anonymity.

CHAPTER 1
THE EARLY YEARS

It was the summer of 1960 when I came into the world, my parents Agnes and Lewis (every one called him Lew) named me Tina. I am the second child, the eldest being my sister Tess. Tess is fifteen months older than me; Mum and Dad thought I was the best baby in the world, just as they did with Tess. I was a normal healthy baby and, as I grew, I got into all sorts of mischief and was a lot cheekier than Tess ever was.

Mum didn't have a good start to life. As a child she contracted a potentially life threatening lung disease, tuberculosis, and she also had to leave school at thirteen to look after Nan. Mum was one of seven children, who all looked after her until the eldest five either got jobs, went to college or got married.

In 1953 Granddad died of a brain tumour. He was forty seven. I was told years later, when I was old enough to understand, that Nan had gone into a deep depression and that's why mum had to look after her. Granddad was not just her husband; he was her life, best friend, soul mate and lover.

She gave up on life after he passed away; she couldn't see a reason to carry on with her life as it was before.

When Tess and I came into the world, the fire that had died within Nan reignited and we gave her the reason to go on. As we were growing up, mum used to tell me and Tess how Nan would never tell our aunts and uncles off if they were naughty. She'd wait for granddad to come home from work and say to him "Brian, have a word with the kids." He'd call them all together and say to them. "You alright kids?" *What a way to be told off.* Nan was a sweet, kind and loving lady, who never had a bad word to say about anyone. She had beautiful, long, dark brown hair forty six inches in length with a streak of grey going over her left ear known as the Mallon streak. Mum had to brush it fifty times a night and put it in a plait before they went to bed. It had a shine to it like a freshly polished mirror.

Money was really tight, so Nan made all my aunts and uncles clothes out of whatever material she could lay her hands on; she was so clever with her hands. She never swore or drank and, before I was born, she had a fall which left her wearing callipers up to her knees on both legs. But with struggling for money and wearing the callipers she never once complained. As we got older, we never asked about the callipers and why she had to wear them; we never heard anyone talking about it either. Tess and I loved her so much she was our Nan so it didn't matter. Anyway, there wasn't anything we could do to upset her, all the love she had for granddad she was giving to us. We were her everything now, she spoilt us rotten and whatever we wanted she would get for us. When we were really naughty, and mum was at her wits end with us, Nan wouldn't let her tell us off , she would come out with the saying "now Agnes they're only children, leave them alone and remember you only have them on loan.

You don't know how long you've got them so make the most out of all you can get. Cherish every moment with them, good or bad." She learned that after almost giving up on her own kids after granddad died. Mum had heard that saying it so many times before she knew it off by heart. Tess and I wanted to spend every waking hour with her. We grew up with an abundance of love from everyone, especially our Nan.

Mum was a pretty lady, five foot four, shoulder length, auburn hair, a fair complexion and blue eyes that sparkled like diamonds in the sunlight, with a smile that was soft and delicate. She was a well built lady, nice and cuddly with a dry sense of humour. However, as we got older when we were naughty we discovered she had a harsh side to her. So, we never made the same mistake twice.

Dad was five foot seven with rugged good looks with and a permanent tan from working outdoors. His eyes were as blue as the as the sky on a clear day. He was quite a muscular man with short dark hair combed back with brylcreme. In 1958 dad lost his job as a bricklayer. He couldn't find another one in the village, so he had to travel miles to try to find another one.

Mum always had his dinner on the table waiting for him to walk through the door just as she did when he was working. After he'd finished his dinner he'd play with us giving us piggy back rides. We'd have fun until it was time for Mum to put us to bed, nothing changed there.

Every Sunday we all went to chapel as did most of the villagers. Mum would put on our Sunday best clothes and they did the same; Dad looked dapper in his suit and mum looked even prettier in her dress, they were a really handsome couple. As they walked down towards the chapel, they would meet up with the other villagers and chat away. Tess would run down with the other children and Nan would push me in my pushchair holding on to it to help her keep her balance. Nan was okay getting down the hill, but she couldn't walk back up it. So after chapel mum would ask one of the neighbours if they'd give her a lift back up, and they were always happy to oblige. Life in the village was good; it was a tight knit community with everyone helping each other, especially in the winter when the snow came with heights of at least six feet and it was impossible to walk in. Most of the men were out at sea fishing for days on end but those who weren't dug tunnels under the snow so that the villagers could get to the shops. The whole community rallied round to make sure the elderly and infirm were looked after. They made sure there was enough food in their cupboards and, if they were unable, they cooked for them. The woman folk kept themselves busy most evenings knitting Fair Isle jumper for their men, especially those who were at sea fishing.

Once a month, all the villagers would get dolled up and go to the local village hall to dance the night away. I wanted to go but Mummy said, "You will have to wait until you're a big girl and all grown up." I said "I can't wait to be all grown up like you mummy." Mum just smiled and said "your time will come soon enough."

There wasn't any trouble in the village. No crime at all it was so peaceful and safe. The local bobby really didn't have much to do, only catching speeding and drunken tourists. We didn't even have a hospital. The nearest one was almost fifteen miles away in Banff. We had a village Doctor, Doctor Jolly; I remember mum saying as we were growing up, "Jolly by name and jolly by nature." There was also a nurse's station so any minor injuries or ailments could be dealt with in the village instead of going to the hospital.

Mum's Uncle Angus owned the local general store. Tess and I loved Mum taking us to the store because he would sometimes give us sweeties. He would always ask mum if we'd been good girls and she would never lie to him. If we'd been naughty, he wouldn't give us any. He was a sweet, kind, loving man who always saw the best in people and never had a bad word to say about anyone; he was just like our Nan in that respect. He treated everyone fairly unless the village kids tried to help themselves to sweets, then he would give them a tongue lashing and a clip around the ear.

The summers were long and hot and mum would to take us down to the beach, the sun popped through the billowy clouds as if to say, "Hello I'm here." It was so hot it felt like coals burning through our clothes. Mum would sit me on a blanket and I'd try to make sand castles with Tess. She'd also throw a ball to us. Tess was okay at catching it but I was still trying to. It was fun and we'd play for hours. Tess would run off to collect muscles, whelks and winkles in her little bucket. She'd splash about in the rock pools so she could cool off. Mum held me so my feet would dangle in the pool so I could do the same. She'd also take us down to the harbour so we could watch the fishing boats come into to dock. We'd watch them unload their catch and I'd never seen so many fish! After they unloaded, they would get their boats ready to set sail again on the next tide. The village became a hive of activity when the boats came into the harbour. The wives, children, and loved ones of the crews rushed to the quayside to greet them. The men being away for days on end in treacherous weather conditions, the relief on all their faces seeing their men and loved ones home safe and sound. The retired fishermen spent their days catching lobsters and crabs or just sitting at the quayside chatting and reading their newspapers, just enjoying the peace and quiet, the only sounds they heard were the seagulls screeching cries.

Dad was still finding it hard to get a job. He had heard that people living down south had a much better life so he started to look for work there. After a while he eventually found a job on the railways repairing the broken tracks with British Rail. Before he could start they sent him to Birmingham to train for the job. Consequently he had to leave Mum up in Scotland until he found us somewhere to live. Until then life was normal. Dad had been away a while when one day out of the blue a lady rang mum and told her that her husband had been staying with her and she was pregnant by him. He wasn't going back to her or the kids. Mum was pregnant with their third child but hadn't yet told dad. That night when he phoned Mum asked him about the other woman and then told him she was expecting. She then gave him an ultimatum, her and the kids or the other woman. Without a second thought, he chose us. He didn't have much of a choice but to move out of her house. He found a B&B, saving all the money he could for a new home for us all. However the money was short lived. Dad started to drink heavily, Mum found out he'd been a drinker since he was thirteen, but he didn't drink much up in Scotland. He went out for a pint or two with his mates and seemed happy with that, however it didn't take him long to squander the money. Mum was quite frugal where money was concerned and managed to save for when we moved. It was hard for her to save, having me and my sister and another one on the way and also needing things for when the new baby arrived. Dad had no idea mum was saving for when we moved. By now, the drink had gotten hold of him that much he was missing some of his visits with us. When he did visit us we, noticed he'd changed. He was a completely different man. He wasn't the daddy or husband we once knew and loved, the soft gentle loving man had gone. He had a temper. A temper he didn't seem to have had before. One we'd never seen. He would lash out at the slightest thing Mum became scared of him, but when we had visitors he'd put on a front, no one knew this man had become an ogre and tyrant and when the visitors left he'd just start lashing out at Mum. When he could be bothered to visit us, Tess and I had to sit and say nothing. Mum did her utmost to keep daddy happy just for our sakes. On one of his visits, Dad found a jar with money in it; the money mum had been saving for when we eventually moved. Desperate for drink, he took most of it and left a small amount. There wasn't enough to even buy food for the new house, let alone anything else we needed for the move. Mum was upset and very angry, but what could she do? He was her husband and the father of her children, all she could do was to start saving again, but this time she left the money with Uncle Angus to keep in his safe, knowing full well dad would never find it there. On his next visit he went straight to the jar and there were only a few pounds in it. He didn't care. He took the lot. Drink was more important to him. Luckily he never knew about the money left with Uncle Angus.

Mum gave me and Tess one penny each spending money. With big smiles on our little faces, she'd take us to the store to buy our sweeties. Angus offered to help, but Mum always refused, being the proud lady that she was. Angus found a way to help her; every time we bought our sweets, he'd put our pennies in the jar instead of the till and he'd also put a little extra in out of his own pocket too. When dad had gone back, Mum went to the shop to see how much she had saved; she had a rough idea and couldn't understand why there was more than she thought there was. She asked Angus, he shrugged his shoulders and said, "Don't know." He could see what was going on between them and couldn't say anything as the last time he said something, Mum turned on him and told him, "It has nothing to do with you," so he helped the only way he knew how to, by helping her save. Angus thought that, once they moved into our new home, things would be different and Lew would change back to the man he used to be. Mum didn't realise that it was the drink that made her husband the ogre and tyrant he now was.

The years had flown by, it was now 1962 and I was still not walking, another thing for Mum to worry about and there was still no signs of us moving. It wasn't long after Dad went back mum gave birth to their first son. Dad always wanted a son, mainly to carry on the family name, but he couldn't be bothered to attend the birth. They named him Robert. When she eventually came home with Robert, Dad made our lives hell. He would shout at us for no reason and, no matter what Mum said or did for him, it was always wrong. He would make her suffer. He would call her all sorts of names, thick and stupid, a moron, a fucking cow and anything else he could think of. He would also hit her for no apparent reason; Mum didn't deserve it, she was everything a wife and mother could be. She pleaded with him to stop drinking but all he could say was, "It's not the drink, it's you, you made me do it." Mum was adamant that once we moved down south and were a family again, things would change for the better and Dad would be the man he once was and not the man he became.

The district nurse, Nurse Blackburn visited every day for a week after Mum brought Robert home, just to make sure he was feeding okay and checking his general wellbeing. Robert was growing and thriving, however, Mum was concerned about me. I was now two years old and couldn't walk, so while Nurse Blackburn was visiting Robert Mum took the opportunity to mention to her about it. She told Mum I was a late developer and I'd walk when I was ready to. Eventually, six months later, I did start walking and one day while I was playing in the front garden Nurse Blackburn was passing and noticed I was wearing a pair of jelly shoes. She knocked on the door to speak to Mum and told her that I shouldn't be wearing those shoes because there was a problem with my feet. I was walking pigeon toed so she told Mum that she must exercise my feet and I must wear Clark's shoes or I may have to wear special shoes with callipers.

Soon after this, Dad contacted Mum and told her he'd finally found a house for us all to live. However, it needed some work doing on it so Mum didn't waste any time in packing and buying the things she needed and leaving enough clothes for us all to wear until the move. She had to think of excuses as to where she got all the new things from so she told dad that her family had given them to her. The family agreed to write message cards for each of the items, knowing he would lash out if he knew Mum had been hiding money. All that was left to buy was the cooker, carpets and fridge which she couldn't get until after we moved in.

Christmas was fast approaching; Mum started to buy and wrap the presents but couldn't pack them just in case we hadn't moved. The next time Dad came home for the weekend, he saw all the boxes had been packed and stacked around the rooms; he asked Mum, "Where are you going with my children?" She tried to explain that they were packed ready for the move but he wouldn't listen and accused her of having someone else and hit her hard. His mood swings were getting worse. She couldn't understand what was happening to the family but most of all to her husband. She had no idea that he had been drinking and it was the drink that changed him. After the incident he went for a walk, something he always did after he lost his temper with Mum. After a few hours, he would return as though nothing had happened. He'd be just like the man she married all those years ago. He went to kiss her it was then she smelt something strange on his breath. She didn't say anything just in case he lost his temper again. As he started to fall asleep on the sofa, she told him she had to pop down to the store for some milk, bread and a few other bits. She knew Angus would be in the store so she asked him, "Has Lew been in?" the fear on Angus's face said it all. "Yes Lew has been in, he tried to buy a bottle of whiskey but I refused to sell it to him." Lew got so upset he did no more than to beat Angus up and helped himself to a bottle. Mum now understood why it was called the demon drink. The villagers were quite religious and the only time they bought whiskey was for medicinal purposes and that was the only time Angus would sell it to them. It was generally sold to the tourists.

Mum thought that, once they moved, she would try to get him off it. Deep down she knew it would never happen, but she lived in hope. When she got home, Dad was awake and started again. He wanted to know where she'd been and who she had been speaking to and what she'd been saying. She reiterated that she'd only gone to the store to get some groceries. After that day Dad wouldn't let her go out by herself and when he went back to work, he had most of his family watching her every move. If she tried to go out, one of them went with her. We found out much later that those people whom we thought were his family weren't, because the village was so small we called everyone aunty and uncle. We never really knew any of his side of the family; we'd seen his Mum a couple of times but didn't really know her. She lived in Aberdeen. He never took us to see her. He lied to mum, just to put the fear of God into her and it worked. He had no reason to *but in his head he did*. Mum found it very hard to be herself and to do things with us while she was constantly being watched. She would say many times "I wish we'd already moved, would we ever move?"The waiting seemed to go on for what felt like a life time. Then out of the blue, he rang her and told her that we would be moving soon, *was this one of his lies, or was he telling the truth for once?* As the conversation went on, Mum's face started to light up. As soon as she hung up she started to busy herself packing the rest of the stuff. She was so excited, the thought of not being watched when she went out and to feel free to go shopping and to take us kids to the park and to be able to relax was a weight off her shoulders. Mum was excited and apprehensive about leaving Scotland, leaving all her friends and family behind, but she knew it would probably be for the best.

CHAPTER 2
THE MOVE

December 12th 1964, was a cold, wet, grey day when we moved down to Oxfordshire. It was really strange for us. We even found the language strange, we had trouble understanding the dialect and I suppose they couldn't understand us either with our Scottish accents. Tess and I didn't understand why there wasn't any sea and sand just lots of buildings to me; it was a dull and unwanting place. I started to cry so Mum asked me what was up, "I want to go back home to Scotland," I told her. Mum cuddled me and said, "This is our home now and we'll be a family again and we will see Daddy every day." Hearing that made me feel a little better. We had trouble settling in, we didn't have any friends yet and no family here, just people we would say hello to in passing.

Christmas in our new home was upon us and mum did the best she could with what little money she had. She tried to make it a good one; we had a few little things wrapped up Mum tried to make it look like we had lots. Christmas in Scotland was great fun. Dad would help us open our presents, he'd play with us while Mum was preparing and cooking the dinner like most, we would have the traditional Christmas dinner. Mum would put all the veggies and potatoes in serving dishes on the table so they could help themselves. Tess and I were too young to do that so Dad put ours on our plates for us. As usual he would carve the turkey and after dinner we would all go to chapel to see the nativity play. Then there would be a sing-a-long of Christmas carols, everything was based on the true Christmas spirit and very much family orientated. The New Year or Hogmanay was for the adults, but in Oxford we didn't have our family or friends to celebrate it with. I kept asking mum "When are we going to see Nan again" all she kept saying was "soon."

Mum didn't know where the churches were, and she wanted us to keep up with our religious upbringing, the closest thing to a church was the Salvation Army. We would go to their Sunday school in the morning for an hour then in the afternoon after lunch we'd go to the main service. We would look forward to going to Sunday school as it was somewhere different to go instead of being stuck in the house, we'd colour pictures of shepherds with their flocks and religious icons and the last fifteen minutes we would have parts of the bible read to us. Dad stopped going to church when he started drinking, *drink was his God now*. I couldn't understand why everything wasn't the same and why he stopped doing things with us? He wasn't the same with us, he didn't play with us anymore, and we never had fun with him like we used to. I thought to myself *why don't you play with us like you used to? It's Christmas, we always had fun when we played with our toys together*. Nothing was anything like the Christmas's up in Scotland. The atmosphere wasn't as relaxed as it used to be. We were also missing our Nan very much and even more so at this time of year. We were still asking when we would see her again, Mum still kept saying, "Soon". Tess started school and she seemed to enjoy it. I was still having trouble understanding why everything was different and why it would be a long time before we saw our Nan again. We also missed all the people we left behind up in Scotland just as much. One day, Dad came home from work, ate his dinner, got changed then told Mum he was going to see his girlfriend. She said to him "Your wife and kids are here, you're not going there anymore." Mum had no idea he was still seeing that harlot. He turned on Mum, hit her hard and called her all the names under the sun, what could she do? Me and Tess were crying, Mum gathered us up into her arms to comfort us and we put our arms around her to comfort her. I kept thinking *why was he like this, what have we done* and *why doesn't he love us anymore?* I was starting to hate him, I stopped calling him Dad. He was just Lew to me now.

Life went on as normally as it possibly could, Lew was at work, Tess was at school and I was at home with Mum and Robert. The garden was quite big so there was plenty of room for us to run around and play. The winter and spring came and went, the long hot summer days were now upon us and so were the school holidays. I loved the holidays because Tess was at home and I had my sister to play with. Mum would put a picnic together and take us all to the park. She would push us on the swings and roundabouts, we'd play ball and there was a paddling pool which we thought was a swimming pool because it looked so big. We'd paddle in it to keep cool, just as we did in the rock pools in Scotland only now I could paddle on my own. We had lots of fun just like we did in Scotland, only without the beach.

Tess and I got on well as children, we played and did all the normal things children of our ages would do, me being five and Tess six. Robert was only three but we made sure he was included in our games so he didn't feel left out. The holidays were coming to an end which meant I would be starting school, I was excited and looking forward to it but also scared at the same time. It was something out of the norm and very different I asked myself, "*Would the other children like me? Would I make friends?*" Mum busied herself getting our clothes ready for school. There wasn't any uniform so mum repaired anything that needed to be sewn and washed and ironed them. She always tried to make sure we were smartly dressed. When it came to how we looked and dressed Mum was a very proud woman.

September 1965, the first day at school and as Mum was walking us there, I started to get a funny feeling in my stomach, a twisting and turning feeling. Mum said, "It was just nerves and it would settle down, I had nothing to be worried about because Tess would be there if I got scared." As we walked through the school gates, all I could see was what looked like a vast ocean of children running around, shouting over each other to be heard. The noise was so over whelming I had to put my hands over my ears to drown it out but that didn't help much. Tess ran off to find her friends. I didn't like that, I felt as though she was leaving me. Mum tried to explain to me that she had her own friends and she played with them every day, but it was difficult for me to understand why? She played with me at home so why not at school?

Mum walked me round to where my classroom was and as we turned the corner there were more children just like me looking scared and apprehensive. I thought I was the only one not sure what to do or where to go. Some were crying wanting to go home and their mothers trying to console them. I stood there looking around, and as I turned I noticed a girl in a corner with her Mum she looked more frightened than I was *bless her*. She was trying to hide behind her Mum, then the teacher came out to take us all into class. We followed with our mothers in tow and I noticed that the girl I'd seen trying to hide behind her Mum was nowhere to be seen so I stopped and told Mum about her. But all mum wanted to do was to get me into the classroom, she thought I was trying to avoid going to school. In the end, I ran off to where we were waiting and she was still there with her Mum still trying to get her into school. She was crying and saying she wanted to go home. Mum was behind me, calling me to go back to the classroom, but I couldn't. I don't know why? I just walked up to the girl and held my hand out to her. We looked at each other for a few seconds, not saying a word, then she took my hand and we started walking towards where our classroom was. Our mothers couldn't believe it they looked at us in amazement. Had I made a friend? Only time would tell.

Soon all my fears dispersed, what was I worried about? I soon got in a routine with school life it seemed so easy at five years old. The girl I helped eventually told me her name was Lucy. She was a bit of a loner and stood in a corner at break times watching the other kids playing. They tried to involve her in their games but she didn't want to know. As soon as I got back into my classroom after break time, I told my teacher about Lucy. He told me she was an only child, I didn't understand what he meant and I thought it was something bad. I was worried about it for the rest of the day. It was time to go home; Mum was waiting outside and as soon as I spotted her, I ran into her arms she gave me a cuddle and then we whipped around the corner to pick Tess up from her classroom. On the way home mum asked us if we both had a good day and what had we been doing. Tess told Mum first what she had done and was full of excitement over something she did. I didn't hear what it was I just went off into a world of my own, it was playing on my mind that Lucy was an only child. When we got home, Mum could see I was worried about something. When she asked what it was I told her about Lucy and what the teacher had said about her. Mum explained that being an only child meant she had no brothers or sisters. As I played in the garden with Robert, I wondered what Lucy was doing, *she must have been lonely playing on her own.*

Mum was really struggling to do everything herself and she got tired very easily *and Lew was as much use as a chocolate tea pot.* She was expecting her fourth child in November. Mid November, Mum gave birth to another girl they named her Marie. By December money was tighter than usual and what she had coming in Lew was drinking away. She had to hide money again otherwise he would have had it. There was only enough money for Mum to buy us some fruit and sweets to put in our Christmas stockings.

The first week of December had come and gone when there was a knock at the front door and when Mum answered it she got one almighty surprise. A few of the neighbours had got together and got us a few presents. Mum didn't realise that people knew what was going on in our home, only one woman knew and that was another Scottish lady she had befriended. Some of the things were second hand and there was one thing each that was new. It didn't matter that we had second hand toys, Mum was so grateful to the neighbours that we had something to open on Christmas day.

Christmas day arrived, we were dreading opening our presents, Lew was drunk as usual and verbally abusing Mum. He wanted to know where the presents had come from, he didn't believe they had come from the neighbours and told mum to throw them away. He wasn't letting his kids have second hand toys. Mum had to hide them while he was at home, we could only play with them while he wasn't there. He was never there for us, if he had been the Dad he used to be then Mum wouldn't have had the need to accept the presents from the neighbours and there wouldn't have been the need for them to rally round thanks to Mum's friend.

One day, Mum told us that we'd been having a visitor and they'd been staying a few weeks. We kept asking, "Who is it mummy?" Mum just smiled at us and said, "Wait and see." The day came and Mum made sure we were all smartly dressed and our hairs were nicely brushed and combed then, off we all went to the train station still wondering who was arriving. As the train pulled into the station, the smoke from the train obscured the passengers alighting from it. As it slowly dispersed, we kept looking to see if we knew anyone. Mum told us to stay where we were and not to move. I stood there still wondering who it could be. The passengers were departing in droves but we still couldn't see anyone we knew. Then all of a sudden, at the very far end of the platform I could see an elderly lady walking slowly in our direction. We got really excited when we realised it was our Nan! We were so happy to see her that we all cried tears of joy. We all ran up to her, she wrapped her arms around us and gave us all the biggest hug we'd ever had. Mum took her bags and carried them to the taxi, Nan had never been on a train or in a taxi before. She was really fascinated that you could get someone to pick you up and take you anywhere you wanted to go. Nan's village was so small there was no need for taxis; everything was in walking distance and if Nan needed a lift the neighbours would oblige.

Nan knew what a big town was like from the odd trips she had to Aberdeen. She didn't like it much, the hustle and bustle of the town, too many people and too big and noisy and in some places dirty, but for us she'd put up with it for a while. I overheard her say to Mum "I will stay as long as I can but I can't give you a time limit." We had to make the best of every day as if it was the last, we didn't know if we would ever see her again. She managed to stay for two weeks before she started to feel home sick and wanted to go. Mum understood but we didn't and when mum told us that Nan was going back to Scotland because she was home sick in all innocence I said to Mum, "she doesn't look sick but if she is we better get the doctor to her." Mum just laughed. The next day, we took Nan to the station and waited with her to make sure she got on the train okay. After all the passengers were on the station master blew his whistle and the train slowly started to move, picking up speed as it reached the end of the platform. We were still waving as the train sped out of sight. As we were walking away all we could do was cry and all mum could do was to comfort us by cuddling and holding us.

CHAPTER 3

THE PASSING OF NAN

As the weeks passed, Mum could see we were still upset and missing our Nan very much so she decided to save some money so she could take up to Scotland the following year for a holiday. Christmas was creeping up fast but, being frugal with money, Mum put a bit aside and told us not to tell Lew because he would take it and spend it on his beloved drink. He found the Christmas money in a jar and asked Mum what it was for, she told him, "for the kid's presents, and she didn't want the neighbours feeling sorry for us and embarrassing her again." All he said was, "They're only kids and they don't need a lot so you won't need all of this," so he took more than half of the money. She knew he'd be back for the rest. Luckily enough he hadn't found the holiday funds. Mum hated lying to him but needs must, she had to for our sakes. What was left she kept in the jar and started a new one and made sure it was well hidden so he wouldn't find I next time. Whatever she saved now wouldn't be enough for Christmas, but if needs be she'd have to delve into the holiday fund. Mum was pregnant again with her fifth child. As it happened she kept some of the baby clothes from when Marie was born, she didn't talk about the holiday just in case we didn't go. She told us Lew had taken the Christmas money and she had to use the holiday money instead but she would try again after Christmas. With all the excitement over the baby the holiday was never mentioned again.

Christmas was here and gone in a flash, we didn't get a lot again, but that was okay. We were really grateful for what we got and we knew Mum tried her best. She was trying to save as much as she could again for the holiday and trying to buy things for the baby. Not knowing if it was a boy or girl she had to get things in pale colours. She knitted cardigans, booties and mittens. It was cheaper to buy wool and knit your own rather than buy ready made from the shops, it would save her some money to put towards the holiday.

As the months past we got even more excited and before we knew it, April was here and the baby was due. The Scottish lady mum befriended, Isobel was her name, asked Mum, "If your husband is the way he is with you, why do you still have his babies?"Mum's answer confused me, I didn't understand what was said, she answered, " What can I do when he comes in drunk and makes me do what he wants?"Back then you just had to put up with it. There was no help available then. *In this day and age it would be called marital rape.* Isobel then understood a lot more about what mum was going through. Out of the corner of her eye she spotted me, oh boy did I know it. For the first time in a very long time I got the sharp end of her tongue. I didn't understand why I was being told off. It was years later that I really understood and after that tongue lashing I always made sure when Isobel visited I'd make myself scarce.

During one of Isobel's visits, Mum went into labour, Isobel phoned the hospital and then Lew but she was shocked at his reply, "That's alright she's had all the others by herself so she can do the same with this one." The look of disgust and anger on Isobel's face said it all, she stayed at Mum's bedside. Lew forgot me and Tess were still in school so he had to come home. Marie and Robert were at one of the neighbours which didn't please him, he thought Mum should have waited until he got home before she went into hospital. *Didn't he stop to think that babies don't wait? Of course he didn't he was too busy drinking and being drunk.*

Mum wasn't in hospital long before Alex came into the world and after a few days, they both came home. Tess and I were all over him trying to get the first cuddle, and it wasn't long before things got back to what we knew as normal. As usual Lew would drink all the money away and then come home and start calling Mum a fucking bastard, a fat cow, a bitch and then he'd start hitting her because his dinner wasn't waiting for him on the table. As the months passed Lew had started on me, Tess and Robert. He didn't hit us but shouted and verbally abused us calling us fucking brats little cunts over the smallest things; because we didn't hang our coats up as soon as we walked in from school or we didn't put our shoes away. It was then Mum told him she was taking us to Scotland for a holiday. She was shocked when he agreed and then said to her, "I will get the tickets." Only so he could dictate when she would go and come back. As it happened that really didn't bother Mum. He wanted to know how long she wanted to go for, " two weeks" she told him. He wasn't happy but agreed to it. He wanted to know everything, where we were staying, who we were going to see, (which he already knew, our Nan.) He still didn't know about the holiday fund and he never found it this time. The weeks turned into months and the summer was now here. He got the tickets and handed her four, she told him she needed six, but he told her the two youngest travelled for free. Mum was angry and upset. If she had known she could have taken us back there sooner. He took us to the station and made sure we got on the train. As the train moved from the platform we all waved to him. The further away from the station we went the more relaxed we all started to become, for the first time in a very long time we'd never felt so relaxed.

After hours of travelling we finally reached our destination, Aberdeen. We were pleasantly surprised to see Uncle Angus waiting there to meet us. Tess and I ran into his arms. He gave us a big hug, at last a kind friendly face, a happy face. He picked up our cases and we followed him to the bus stop, it'd been a very long time since we'd been on a bus Robert and Marie had never been on one before and they loved it, they played and laughed until we reached the stop we needed to get off at. When we got off the bus, Nan was waiting to meet us. Tess, Robert and me ran up to her. We couldn't wait for one of her cuddles and she bent over and gave us a big one. Marie and Alex were apprehensive, they had never met Nan before and went very shy. We arrived at Nan's house she had what Mum called delicate sandwiches all laid out on the table there were sandwiches cut in triangles with the crusts cut off, homemade scones with jam and cream and we had orange squash whilst the adults had cups of tea. We all sat round the table and ate until we couldn't eat anymore, except for Mum. She sat in Nan's big comfy chair smiling. It was so nice for her to see us happy and she didn't mind all the chatter from us, she usually told us to be quiet when adults were talking. It was different this time. She was so happy to see us like we used to be, everything was so nice and relaxed. We had so much fun the time passed too quickly it was time for bed. We got ready, Nan gave us a big kiss and cuddle and then Mum took us up to bed. It didn't take us long to go off to the land of nod. The next morning, when we woke up, Tess and I were covered in spots; we both had German measles' Nan put a quarantined sign on the front door so that people would know not to call. Robert, Marie and Alex were only allowed to play in the garden, they weren't allowed to play with any other kids. By the time the spots cleared and we weren't infectious anymore, the holiday had come to an end. It wasn't much of an holiday but at least we saw our Nan. When it was time to go home, Tess and I cried, we wanted to stay with Nan but Mum said we had to go home because school would be starting soon and she had to get everything ready for us. The previous year Tess moved up to the junior school and now it was my turn. Robert was going to start infant school but Marie and Alex was still too young to go to school.

The first day at the new school was extremely daunting and much bigger than I expected it to be, I didn't like my teacher, Miss Bloom, all the older kids called her "old Bloomer."Every now and then she would hear one or two of them saying it. She had such a sharp tongue and soon had them in tears. One day Mum arranged for one of the other mothers to pick us up, she was a nice lady but I did not want to go with her, she wasn't my mum. Eventually she persuaded me to go with her. When we got home, Mum was there she'd been crying. At first I thought Lew had been home and started on her again. We didn't say anything to her we just carried on with what we normally did. After a while, she called us into the kitchen we sat at the kitchen table thinking it was teatime and then Mum sat down we could tell there was something wrong, I couldn't understand why there were only three of us around the table? The three of us sat there what seemed like hours, then all of a sudden! Mum said, "There's something I have to tell you." Then she went quiet again. She was trying to find the right words but the only words she could find was, "Nan has gone to be a star in the sky." We all looked at each other trying to work out what she was trying to tell us. We had never heard that saying before. She could see we didn't understand, she had to find another way. It was then she remembered everything we had been taught in church so she started again. "You know God loves everyone?" *we just nodded* and sometimes he comes and gets someone," *we just looked at each other,* "He decided it was her turn to go and see him so your Nan has gone to heaven to be an angel." We then knew what she was trying to say and why she'd been crying. She told us that she'd have to go back to Scotland to say goodbye and Lew would be looking after us. We started crying, Mum thought it was because of Nan but it wasn't. We wanted to go with her we really didn't want to stay with him. She told us she didn't have a choice it had to be that way, but she wouldn't be gone that long three days at the most. There was nothing we could say or do. Two weeks later it was time for her to go she said, "You all make sure you be good kids while I'm away, I'll be home before you know it." We all took her to the station to wave her off. We had tears in our eyes. We tried to hide them from Lew; if he saw the tears he would have hit us just for crying. We couldn't let Mum see him do that while she was leaving, she was upset enough over losing her Mum and leaving us with that devil incarnate without seeing him hit us for showing emotion.

Over the next few days we tried to be as good as we could. We played in our bedrooms, tidied up after ourselves but nothing we did was good enough for him. One night he wanted to go out so he got a baby sitter for us. When he came home he was so drunk he could hardly walk, he made so much noise he woke me, Tess and Robert. Luckily enough Marie and Alex slept through it. We heard him tell the sitter he'd pay her the following day, as he was stumbling up the stairs and passing our bedroom I could hear him say, "She's not getting a penny out of me for looking after those brats."

I thought to myself that's not fair I'm going to pay her. I knew where mum kept the money, the problem I had was getting it to the sitter without him seeing. I didn't think Mum would mind under the circumstances if I explained to her when she came home. The next day he popped out into the back garden, this was my chance, I had to be quick! I managed to get a few pounds and put it in my pocket, I now had to find a way to give it to her. All of a sudden there was a knock at the front door and it was the sitter wanting her money, they started to row when he told her she wasn't getting it. While they were rowing I asked him if I could play out in the front garden. I was surprised when he said yes. I knew it'd only be for a short time while he was rowing with the sitter, he wouldn't normally let us play in the front although Mum did when he wasn't there. He only said I could go in the front for show while the sitter was at the door. Eventually the row stopped and he shut the door in her face, this was my chance. As she started to walk pass me I said, "Hello." Luckily enough she stopped and started to talk to me, I then passed her the money hoping he wasn't spying through the curtains. I told her I was sorry I didn't have more, she said. "It was enough," and thanked me. All of a sudden I heard the sound I was dreading, he was calling me in. While we were sat having our tea he just sat there staring at us and mumbling something. We couldn't understand what he was saying, then all of a sudden he slammed his fist on the table and said, "It's your fault I can't go out, I wished you'd never been born." *I thought to myself why is God letting this happen to us, are we really bad, when is Mum coming home?* A few days later Mum came home. The sadness we all felt while she was away melted like snow on a spring day, the smiles we all had was like the sun beaming down on a summers day. Before Mum got her coat off we were asking all sorts of questions about anything and everything, but most of all about the family up there. After things had settled down, Mum asked us how things had been with Lew. He was still in the same room as us all, what could we say? We said things were fine out of fear of what he'd do to us. As soon as he went out I told Mum everything, especially how he refused to pay the sitter. I told mum I took the money to pay the sitter. She wasn't happy about it but understood the reason I did it, even to this day I don't know whether she was mad because I'd taken the money or the reason I had to do it. It wasn't long before things got back to how they always were.

1967 soon became 1968 and Lew's mood swings became much worse. He was starting on us more than normal. Mum tried to intervene but as usual he would lash out at her. Christmas had come and gone again, as usual we were grateful for what we got. As Mum did every year she tried her best. Another year over and like all the other years we hoped the next one would be better. 1968 was much of how all the other years had been. Lew still the drunken bastard and bully he's always been. In the August Mum realised she was pregnant with her sixth child.

1969 was upon us and in the April Mum gave birth to another girl and named her Ann. The following year things changed for the good. Mum's sister Margaret came to live with us. For some reason she needed somewhere to live and rumour had it that she left Scotland because she was pregnant. *It wasn't the thing back then to have a child out of wed lock,* but we didn't know if that was the real reason or not. Lew didn't like the idea of her staying with us but had to put up with it. Only Uncle Angus knew what he was really like and he wouldn't have told anyone about it. Lew put on an act while Margaret was around; he was all sweetness and light. One night I overheard him tell Mum Margaret had to get her own place. Unfortunately he was right, we were overcrowded, Mum wasn't stupid she knew once Margaret left there would be no stopping him again. Aunty Margaret had been with us for a few months now when we found out she was expecting and was due in December, *was this the reason she left Scotland?* We still didn't know. It was obvious now that she had to get a place of her own.

The next day Mum took her to the council offices for her to put her name on the list for a house. When they got back home Mum told Lew until the council found a house for Margaret she would have to stay with us a wee bit longer. Lew still wasn't happy about it, *but he was never happy about anything,* he still had to keep up the act. We were overjoyed that Aunty Margaret was staying a wee bit longer. Well it was more of a relief although we loved her being here with us. However we knew we would be relatively safe while she was here with us. Unfortunately it wouldn't last forever so we'd have to make the best of every day she was with us.

Mum was still hiding money, again another summer was approaching, and Mum wanted to take us out on day trips. Tess was growing fast and after the holidays she'd be starting senior school, so there was her uniform to buy. The only help out there was for single mothers on benefits and Mum was neither of those. Money was tighter than ever so Mum had to get a job. The money helped a little but, as usual, Lew was taking most of it for his beloved drink, that's about the only thing that stayed the same. While we were at school Mum helped an elderly lady with whatever she needed doing; washing, ironing cleaning, shopping and anything else that the lady needed. Margaret had three little ones while Mum was working and she eventually got her own house. But she came round every day so Mum could keep her job. Mum thought that when Margaret's baby arrived she would have to give up her job; Marie would be starting school so it would only be Alex and Ann to look after. There was still a while yet before Margaret had her baby so Mum carried on working and saving. The summer holidays were now here so Mum started to sort out the money on the kitchen table to see if she saved enough to do what she needed to do. Top of the list was Tess's school uniform, and school shoes for those of us who went to school, these were top priority. As Mum was counting the money she didn't notice Lew had walked in. *I would have loved to see the look on his face when he saw all that money on the table, but I was playing in the garden.* He was furious that Mum had hid the money and lied about it, but as the saying goes *needs must as the devil drives*, and he was the devil. Mum tried to explain to him that the money was for the school uniforms and shoes and day trips, all he could say was, "They don't need day trips and their shoes would have to last longer," then he took most of the money for his demon drink. The rest of the money had to be spent before he came back so she arranged with Margaret to look after us all while she popped into town. He knew he'd taken too much, there wasn't enough to get Tess's uniform, the only things she bought new were her shirts and tie. The jumpers and skirts came from the second hand shop. After Mum had washed and ironed and sewn any little tears in them they looked brand new. There were a few more weeks before went back to school. Mum managed to save enough from her job to get three new pairs of shoes. Mine had to wait until later because I had to have Clarks and they were the most expensive out of the lot. Marie's birthday was on its way so she had to save and hide money for that.

Another Christmas was also on its way; each week mum would buy presents and keep them at aunty Margaret's so Lew didn't see them. Margaret was getting close to her due date and the last thing Mum wanted was her to have the baby Christmas week. If she did how was she going to get the presents? Mum wasn't a selfish person by nature but on this occasion it was fear making her that way; fear that we wouldn't get our presents on the day and fear that if he had seen them she would of got a beating for spending the money he could have had for his drink. On December the twelfth Margaret had a baby girl. She named her June it was also six years to the date that we moved to Oxford. By the time Christmas came Margaret and June were home, *thank God*. Mum was so relieved that she could now stop worrying about the presents, but she still hadn't got over the passing of our Nan and had to carry on regardless.

Despite the fact Margaret didn't come round very often now she had June, she still looked after Alex and Ann Mum dropped them off to her house, it was a lot easier to do that rather than Margaret get a new born ready to take out into the cold. If Mum had enough time they'd have a cuppa and a chin wag before she went off to her job. Me, Tess and Robert were now of an age where we could help Mum a lot more. Robert and I dropped Marie off at infant school and then we walked across the playground to our classrooms in the junior part of the school. Tess walked to school it was a wee bit further than the junior school.

Little did I know that this was going to be the start of my nightmare! It all started one day in early February I had just got in from school with Robert and Marie. I was only ten, Mum was in the kitchen preparing the evening meal like she always did. Alex and Ann were in the garden playing. As I walked through the house to put my things away I became very uneasy. I didn't know why? After I put my coat away and turned round, there he was sat in his chair, he asked me, "Where have you been."

I answered, "School," he asked me again, "where have you been?" I didn't understand why he kept asking me that question. I didn't know I was five minutes late and he wanted to know who I was with. I tried to tell him I wasn't with anyone but he didn't believe me he called me a liar. He called Mum through from the kitchen. By now Mum was so frightened of him she'd drop everything at his command. He got out of his chair and walked over to me then turned to Mum and said "You know I don't like liars," all she could do was put her head down as he turned back and hit me hard across the face. The stinging and burning sensation was horrendous. My face felt as though it was on fire. Until then he had never hit any of us kids. He thought he'd teach me a lesson thinking I'd lied to him. He asked me again, what could I tell him? As always I'd come straight home from school he hit me again and sent me to my room and told me I wasn't getting any tea until I told the truth. It didn't matter what I said he would have still done the same. I could hear children playing outside, so I looked out of the window, he shouted upstairs, "If you're anywhere near the window you will get it again."

Because Tess was in senior school she finished a bit later than I did, so when she got home she came straight upstairs to change out of her uniform. She wanted to know why I wasn't playing out. I told her what happened and she said, "I'll try to get you something to eat." She didn't return. By the time bedtime came around I was already asleep. I woke up in the early hours starving. I couldn't sneak downstairs, some of the stairs creaked and he would hear me. The morning seemed to be forever coming then Mum shouted us all to get up. By the time I got downstairs he'd already left for work so Mum made me a big breakfast, cereal, toast and egg, I couldn't eat it all but she didn't mind, although money was tight she never forced us to eat everything.

The next day after school I went to collect Robert and

Marie. I told them to hurry. Just as we got to the school gates I saw Mum waiting. She warned me he was home again but I didn't care Mum was with me and she would know I didn't meet anyone. He didn't believe anyone. He was permanently drunk. After all the years of drinking he started to get more and more paranoid and violent as I was about to find out when we got home. He hadn't forgotten about the previous night, he started again about meeting people but this time he asked me who mum had met. I stood there in disbelief. The bastard had sent mum to meet us then accused her of meeting a man. She told him she hadn't but just like me he didn't believe her then he went to hit her and missed and hit me instead, I just happened to be in the way of impact, then the bastard accused me of interfering he took his belt off and made me bend over. Mum tried to stop him but he just carried on hitting me with it. My brothers and sisters kept out of his way and when he'd finished belting me he'd ask again about the man Mum was supposed to be meeting. Every night was the same and because I didn't say what he wanted t hear he'd hit me and send me to bed with no tea. *Looking back I think he was looking for an excuse to break my spirit just like he had with mum.* Tess kept telling me to lie. If I had, what would he have done to mum? He'd already broken her and we were taught in church that it was a sin to lie.

Over the period of seven years that we lived here in Oxford I'd seen the sparkle slowly draining out of Mum's eyes. There was only sadness in them and I wasn't going to make things worse for her, not if I could help it. Over the months there were more accusations, then he accused us of plotting something, *God knows what he thought we were plotting.* With Tess, me and Robert being the eldest we seemed to get it from him all the time. I couldn't wait until September to move schools as I'd be out of the way. The months passed slowly and my eleventh birthday wasn't far off, *what sort of birthday was I going to have? Only time would tell.* He was drinking more money than he normally did out of his wages, he was giving Mum barely enough to get what we need in food, he even made her hand over all her wages from her little job and he was still accusing her of having an affair. I wouldn't have blamed her if she was. Bloody hell Mum didn't have enough time in the day to do everything she had to do let alone have an affair, but he was too stupid, thick and drunk to know that. My birthday came and went. Mum, bless her as usual, did her best and managed to get me a little present but no card. None of us got cards that year. Mum thought a present would be better than a card, she couldn't afford both.

The school was putting on a end of year play and they were auditioning. I couldn't be bothered to, I was leaving so as far as I was concerned what the hell. Because I didn't audition, the teachers told me I had to be in the choir. Through the rehearsals the teachers chose me to do a solo despite the fact I didn't want to. During the production all the choir had to sing Windmill in Old Amsterdam. We practiced so much I began to hate the song. All that was going through my mind for weeks were the words *I saw a mouse where? There on the stair, right there! A little mouse with clogs on, well I declare! Going clip-clipperty –clop on the stair, oh yeah.* Even to this day I can't stand that bloody song. When the audience thought the show had ended, I ran off stage and did a quick change into a white robe with wings attached. With my blonde curly hair and blue eyes I looked quite angelic, I then came back on stage and did my solo, Ave Maia. The audience gave us all a standing ovation.

Yet again the summer holidays were upon us. Just like all the other years Mum did her best to make them happy times for us, and as she did with Tess she had to get some of my uniform from the second hand shop. The shirts were Tess's hand me downs as the only uniform she could afford to buy was for Tess as she was getting bigger and her uniform would be more expensive. I didn't mind because of the situation, none of us kids expected much from Mum, we had tons of love from her which was enough. As for Lew, we came to the conclusion he never really loved us and we were just in the way and he was that way because of mum's family. Mum had a lot of family back in Scotland; looking back I think Lew behaved himself and was the perfect husband and father because he was surrounded by all our family. He didn't have much family up there and we didn't see much of them, I asked myself *"was it all a front being the doting and loving dad?*

We always had fun in the holidays, this year was no different. We went to the park, had walks in the countryside which we all loved and we felt free and relaxed we were free to run wild, play and make as much noise as we wanted to. Now and again Mum would put together a picnic for us all. The holidays came to an end oh so quickly, and it was back to school.

I found the new school hard. It was a lot bigger than the Junior School and we had to go from classroom to classroom depending on which lessons we were having. I thought to myself *why couldn't the teachers come to our classroom instead of us going to theirs?* I was getting bullied at school because of Tess. She was a big mouth bitch and told some of her friends that my clothes were not only second hand but also some of her hand me downs. She was overheard by some of the other kids, word soon got around and the school bullies were out in force. The comments they made like Second Hand Rose from the song of the same name, everyone shouted when they saw me, they came up to me, pushed me and laughed in my face. Tess didn't do or say anything to stop them; she just let it go on. I tried to ignore it and carry on as normal as possible. I never told Mum, she had enough to deal with. Lew and the two little ones were at home, so the last thing she needed was me complaining. Tess did nothing to make it better, it went on for months.

The Christmas break was here thank God. I was more than relieved no more bullies. I was hoping that after the break they would have forgotten about it. Things were getting worse at home. Mum always had new marks on her and we had to spend most of our time in our bedrooms playing quietly so we didn't disturb him as he either watched football or horseracing on the television. Now the bastard started gambling on the football pools every week and also the horses as well as his beloved drink.

When I got back to school after Christmas, the bullies started again. This time I told a dinner lady, she said "I'll keep an eye on them," but never did. One day, as I passed Tess and her friends, I overheard her telling them what she got for Christmas. She was oblivious that I was so close to her that I could hear everything she was saying to them. She told them that she got presents that were more expensive than they actually were. She was in with the In Crowd and she wanted it to stay that way. She was a bloody liar; she told them a pack of lies. I wondered how she would feel if I told her friends the truth. As I started to move away from them, I saw the bullies heading towards me. I quickly changed direction, so much for me hoping they'd forget and so much for the dinner lady keeping a look out. This time it was just verbal. One of them said "we'll see you after school" I had a feeling it wasn't going to be verbal this time. The bell rang for end of day and I ran like a bat out of hell to avoid them all. The following day they spotted me going into the toilet block, they came in after me and that's when I got it! By the time I walked out of there I was covered in cuts and bruises and, to add salt to the wounds, one of the girls had gone and told a teacher I had started on them. I couldn't prove I hadn't, however, the teacher had her doubts because I was marked and they had no marks on them at all. Tess was put to the test by her mates to find out where her loyalties lay so she told the teacher it was me who started it so she could stay in with the In Crowd. The bastards knew they had got me; they knew they could keep bullying me and get away with it because no one would believe me if I reported it.

CHAPTER 4

THE ABUSE

The school sent a letter home with Tess explaining everything that happened and how I was to blame. Mum asked me exactly what had happened, I explained it all to her from the very beginning and Tess admitted I was telling the truth; she didn't have a choice but to be honest with her. Mum hid the letter so Lew wouldn't find it; he was like a volcano ready to erupt and if he found it he would have certainly erupted. He did find the letter while he was searching for money *I don't know why Mum didn't dispose of it.* He erupted, swearing at Mum and also gave her one almighty smack across the face for not telling him about it. After all she was trying her best to protect us because she knew what he'd do. After he'd read it he shouted for me and Tess to come to him. He wanted to know what was going on in school and when we told him all he could do was to call us "liars" and told Tess to stop protecting me by lying for me, he then sent her out of the room. I stood there trying to convince him I wasn't lying but he still wouldn't accept it. He took off his belt and belted me hard with it quite a few times saying, "You go to school to learn not to fight."

At school the next day, when I was changing for P.E, the teacher noticed I had numerous bruises on me. She pulled me to one side and asked me how I got them, what could I say? If I had told the truth it would have made things worse at home so after a long hesitation I told her I was play fighting with my brothers and fell off the side of the bed. I suspected she didn't believe me but she didn't have much of a choice but to. Sometimes I wished she hadn't taken what I said as the truth at face value. I think if I didn't have any siblings things may have been different, but who knows? Between home and school I was living a nightmare. It didn't matter what I did, I copped it from both. My friend Lucy whom I first met in infant school who wouldn't say boo to a goose moved up schools with me. As she got older, she came out of her shell more and more and, by the time she reached senior school, she was a different Lucy, so full of confidence. Although we were still best mates Lucy had her own circle of friends and I had mine. She also noticed the bruises and came over just as the teacher was asking me about them and overheard what I was saying. Lucy knew I was lying and in no uncertain terms told me so. She also said I should speak up for myself. The school bullies threatened her and told her that if she didn't stay away from me she'd get the same as what I got. Lucy surprised me by how strong she was, *I was nowhere near as strong as her*. She called their bluff. Because she stood up to them, they left us alone in school. After school was a different matter when I was on my own. Lucy had to catch the bus home, she lived further away than I did. Her parents insisted she caught it to make sure she got home safely. Night after night I tried to get out of the gates before the bullies did. Sometimes I would manage it and was safe, but the times I didn't and they caught up with me they would all circle around me so I couldn't escape. I looked around for Tess but she was nowhere to be seen. Oh! She made sure she was out of the way and on her way home, *what a coward*. It took the kids that didn't know me to help. What they didn't know was they were actually saving me from two beatings. If I went home with new cuts and bruises Lew would give me another beating. At times I wished I'd never been born, I kept thinking, *why is God allowing this to keep happening to me?*

As the months passed I slowly spent less and less time with Lucy, I kept telling her I wanted to be alone, eventually she got together with her circle of friends at school and left me alone. I didn't want it to be that way but she was asking too many questions, "Is everything alright at home?" I felt she was getting too close to the truth, I said, "Of course it is." I thought *when are all these lies going to stop?* By the end of the year I was all alone. Between Lew and the bullies my spirit was well and truly broken, I knew there was no help for me. Mum tried but she knew if I told anyone about what was going on in our house there was no telling what he would do. Mum stood up in front of him on a few occasions and took a beating for me. He loved the control he had over us; however, he never started on the three younger ones. The only time Tess and Robert got a lashing was if they did something wrong in the house, which wasn't very often. At times I hated them especially Tess, *why is it always me and not them?* I kept thinking to myself.

One day the Head Teacher called me into his office. He told me he wanted a little chat, his little chats felt like the third degree. He kept asking me questions about my home life and I kept telling him everything was fine. What could I say? I couldn't tell him the truth. No matter how many times I told him things were fine he kept badgering me and in the end I just sat there and stared out of the window until he gave up, knowing he wasn't getting anywhere. He told me to go back to class, this wasn't going to be the end of it and at least I'd be more prepared next time whenever that was going to be.

After school the bullies were waiting for me. They knew I'd been called into the heads Office and they wanted to know what I said and why I said it. I told them I'd said nothing but they didn't believe me and, by the time I got home, I had a cut lip and a black eye. There was no way I could hide a black eye and I knew when I got home I would be in for it from Lew. I told Mum what had happened but unfortunately, there wasn't a lot she could do. I went to my room shaking with fear, not knowing if he'd come up and beat me. Every time I heard footsteps coming up the stairs I felt sick to my stomach *was it him?* No it was just the others coming up to get changed. I stayed in there as long as could, but at some point I would have go down for my tea, Mum thought of a way to keep me in my room at least for the night. I had a little bit of homework to do so she told him I was doing that and I'd be eating in my room. I managed to drag it out so I wouldn't have to face him. Thinking I'd be most of the night doing it, he left me alone. I got away with one night which gave me and Mum plenty of time to think of an excuse for the following night. Tess came up with the idea of hiding my black eye with foundation cream if it was applied properly, *anything was worth a try*. The next morning before I went off to school we put it on to see if it would work. It sort of did. Some of the teachers told me to wash my makeup off; I screwed my face in disgust at the word make up and told them it was disgusting and I'd never wear that stuff. It took me all day to convince them I wasn't wearing any. It had crossed my mind that if the teachers had clocked it, would Lew? That was the big question. When I got home I reapplied it and put it on thin in the places that didn't need it and a little thicker around the eye hoping he wouldn't notice. It worked for a while but not long enough for the bruising to completely fade. He went to slap me across the face, I had no idea what for,(*even to this day I still don't know why)* and some of the foundation came off on his hand. He went totally berserk and told me to go and wash it off. He didn't want any of us wearing makeup, and then he saw what was left of the bruising. He asked me in an angry tone "How did you get that?" Before I could answer him Mum spoke up and told him that I'd walked into a door, him being a drunk had its advantages at times. He was so drunk he believed her after she explained to him why we never told him. I had no idea what she said to him, but know I'd have to be more careful not to get anymore bruises on my face, *easier said than done.* I didn't choose to get beat up, but what was I supposed to do Say, "hold on a minute, don't hit my face."

Mum was still working for the old lady, we never knew her name, she was just known as the old lady. As always mum scrimped and saved what she could, another Christmas was on its way. It was no different from all the other years, but we always tried to have fun. Before we knew it 1972 was with us. As we did every year we hoped the New Year would be better than all the other years and hoped things would change for the good, but it didn't. We went back to school, Mum carried on working. A few months later when we returned home from school, there was no sign of Mum. He was there like a bear with a sore head. We didn't know if we should ask, he could tell what we were thinking, he just looked at us and said "The silly bitch has got herself arrested for stealing and she's at the police station." Mum would never steal, we all knew that, he carried on "the stupid cow she worked for has accused her of stealing a vase and some other things that were probably cheap, so get used to it, because you won't be seeing your mum for a long time." Being young we believed him, however, the next morning when we got up she was there. I just stood and stared at her, it was as though she was reading my mind so she got us all together and told us what had happened. *This was about the only thing he told the truth about.* Mum told us she didn't do it, we already knew that, she wasn't a thief. He had to start on her, wanting to know where the money was that she got for the items. She kept telling him she didn't do it but he didn't believe her. He got his coat on and headed for the front door. Just as he was about to open it he turned around and said to her, "Never mind, you'll be locked up soon, and you know what happens in prison?" All Mum could do was cry. She didn't even know if she was going to be charged, she was really worried. She knew nothing about prisons, and why would they send her to one? She'd done nothing wrong. You would have thought he would have supported her, but as usual, he was just out for himself. Nothing and nobody mattered to him and he made sure she knew it and told her how he felt each and every day. As the days passed Mum was hoping it was the end of it and no more was going to be done. Then it came, the letter she was dreading, the court summons. Mum had to appear in court, she couldn't afford a solicitor so the court appointed one for her. He was useless and mum was found guilty and sentenced to eighteen months for a crime she didn't commit. She probably would have gotten off if she would have had the money to pay for a decent solicitor. Lew refused to go to court with her so she had to face it on her own, he said to her, "You deserve everything you get and how can you call yourself a mother?" He had room to talk, how on earth could he call himself a father? He was totally convinced she was guilty. After all the years they had been married, he should have known she wasn't capable of anything like that.

Mum was sent to Holloway women's prison first; this one was for the more hardened criminals, murderers and the likes, it wasn't a good experience for her and she never told us why. *I suppose it's not a good experience for anyone.* About a month later she was transferred to an open prison in Stoke on Trent. Stoke was more for petty criminals and much more relaxed. We were told we couldn't go to see Mum in either prison. I don't know if it was him being a bastard and not wanting us to see her or if it was Mum being considerate and not wanting us to see her in prison. The first month she was away, liver onions, mash and gravy was on our plates every single night. It was cheap to buy and that was all he could Cook. He made sure he had the majority of the liver; we didn't get much of it. He was a man and he thought he should have had the lion's share. He seemed to think just because we were kids we didn't need a lot to eat. That was him all over, thinking of number one. *Looking back I didn't realise just how selfish someone could be.* If we didn't eat it all, he wouldn't let us leave the table. We'd all had enough to last us a life time, even to the point we all got to hate it. Me, Tess and Robert worked out, that if we got some tissue and wiped our mouths after each mouthful, we could spit the liver into it and hopefully he wouldn't see what we were doing. *Lucky for us he didn't see.* I was twelve and Tess was thirteen. We were doing home economics in school so we decided that we would do the cooking. We weren't sure exactly what we were doing. We sort of remembered how to cook a steak pie and cottage pie from the lessons we had, the rest of the week was pot luck. We borrowed a basic cook book from school and wrote down some of the recipes, but he still had to have his liver and he still had to make us suffer. You could tell by our faces at least one of us was going to bring it up. *Even to this day I can't face liver.*

He only visited Mum twice, the only regular visitor she has was Isobel. She visited every two weeks and kept her informed on how we were doing which wasn't much because Lew made sure she was kept at arm's length. The only place we were allowed to go was school, and very rarely the local shop. Apart from that we had to either play in the back garden or the house. On the occasions we went to the local shop if Isobel saw us she would ask us how we were. What could we say? "Everything was fine and the little ones were well." All I wanted to do was to tell her that he was a useless, selfish bastard and a tyrant but, unfortunately I couldn't say anything. Even if I could have, what could Isobel do? Mum had enough to deal with trying to adjust to life behind bars without having to worry more than she already was about us.

One day things started to change; Lew let Tess go into town with her friends. Were things changing for the good? I was about to find out that wasn't going to be the case. Me and Robert were playing in the back garden with the younger ones because he was trying to do something and needed my help. He called me upstairs to his bedroom, I didn't think anything of it but as I was going up the stairs I was wondering what he needed my help with. But as I walked into the bedroom I froze on the spot. I wasn't expecting to see what I saw, he was sat on the bed in nothing but his Y fronts. He called me over to him I shook my head in defiance.

He stared at me and told me that if I didn't go over to him, he would make me suffer the consequences and so would the others. I had no alternative but to do what he asked. He patted the bed at the side of him for me to sit down then he grabbed hold of my hand and forced it down the front of his pants and told me to stoke IT. I didn't want to do it; he said, "Do it or I'll call Ann up here." She was only three; I couldn't and wouldn't allow him to do that to her. As this thing was getting hard I could feel my stomach churning, I wanted to be sick. All that was going through my mind was *if I didn't do it he would get Ann up here. I couldn't let this happen to her or any of the others.* I had to try to protect them from this evil bastard, I didn't have a choice. I kept thinking *why is he doing this to me?* This went on once a week for quite a few weeks. I knew which day it would be when he let Tess out with her friends. I never knew which day it would be until the day came, I'd be on edge every day, I didn't want to come home wondering if this is the day he'd let Tess out, my stomach would churn I'd feel sick, I would have sooner had the bullies beat me up everyday rather than go home to what he had in store for me. After a while he started to touch my private parts. I objected but it did no good, he didn't care. He was only interested in his own gratification. He said to me, "You're a big girl and this is what big girls do." I was a child, a twelve year old child! Lew started to get more daring, moving from once a week to twice a week. Even with Tess in the house, he kept making me do it to him. He told Tess to make the dinner so that she'd be kept busy and out of the way. Yet again I was called upstairs. I never thought for one minute that he'd do anything with Tess or any of the others in the house. He knew none of them would venture upstairs, they were all too scared of him. He did a good job of making sure they all knew what was expected of them and the main thing was to stay out of his way. We hadn't seen Aunty Margaret since Mum went to prison; and she knew she'd be unwelcome in our house so she stayed away. Each day I kept hoping she would knock on the door, but that was a long time coming.

Every time we saw Isobel she always asked, "Is everything alright?" As always I replied, "Yes." My life had now become one lie after another through no fault of my own. I had to keep lying to protect my brothers and sisters and I hoped and prayed he wasn't doing those things to them as well as to me. Only time would tell. Not one of them ever asked me any questions, *did they know?* And I never said anything to them, what could I say? If I told anyone I wouldn't have been believed, things like that didn't happen. We'd never heard of anything like that, and even if someone would have believed me he would have wriggled his way out of it. He kept carrying on touching me and expecting me to do the same to him when the opportunity arose which it did quite often. I kept objecting but it didn't make a blind bit of difference, he still forced me and it was hurting me his hands were so rough they felt like sandpaper, he didn't care about hurting me. He didn't care about what he was doing knowing it was wrong and every time he did those things to me I felt contempt for him.

One day things really changed. Aunty Margaret eventually came round and asked Lew if it was okay if all the kids went round to hers for our tea. He wanted to know how long we'd be gone she said, "About a couple of hours." A sly grin came on his face with a look as though he'd just thought of something, of course he said, "Yes." He told her that I wasn't allowed to go because I'd been naughty. All I could do was cry. Aunty Margaret thought it was because I wasn't allowed to go, but I knew the real reason. After they'd all gone he went around the house locking all the doors so there was no way of me getting out. It didn't take a genius to work out what was coming and I was no genius. I had no way of stopping him, nowhere to hide and no point in shouting because all the neighbours were out either at work or shopping.

He came into the living room and stood by the door, there was a creepy smile on his face, he told me to go into the kitchen. I wasn't expecting that, however, it did make me wonder what he was up to. I had to do what he told me to. As I walked in there I noticed he'd closed the curtains. I was really scared now. He sat me on the table and started to talk to me, he said "It's about time you become a woman." I thought to myself *I am only girl, it would be a few more years before that happened so what the hell is he going to do?* He stood up and walked over to me and stroked my hair. He had never done that before. I became extremely uneasy more than usual and even more scared. He asked me to take my shorts and T shirt off, I said "No." He did no more than to take off his belt and hit me across my legs. It stung like hell and made me cry even more than what I was already was. He told me to do what I was told otherwise I would get another one. There wasn't much of a choice so I decided I would rather have the belt so I said, "No" again. But this time he didn't hit me, he said, "Next time I see your Mum I will tell her you've been sleeping around." *How could he think of lying to Mum and tell her something like that knowing it to be untrue?* He left me with no choice. I couldn't let him tell Mum something like that, I didn't know if she would have believed him or not. I did what he said and bent over the kitchen table. He then told me I was about to become a woman. With no more said he inserted his fingers inside me, it hurt me so bad I was about to scream when he put his hand over my mouth and told me it was useless because there was no one about. I didn't realise until after he had finished with me and he was washing himself down that it just wasn't his fingers he put inside me. The bastard had raped me. He had gone from touching to having full sex with me, not once but twice. Then there was a knock at the door, *thank God*. It was Aunty Margaret bringing the rest of the kids back. If they hadn't have come back when they did I reckon Lew wouldn't have stopped. I was so numb and very sore, I could still smell the stale whiskey and tobacco from his breath. Tess asked me why the door was locked. I told her I didn't know.

He was spending a lot of time at home. Why wasn't he working? Did he leave his job or was he sacked for drinking? I don't know. I don't know if Mum knew either. After that day at every opportunity he would force me to have sex with him. There were times when I was playing out and he would call me in even though the rest of the kids were playing in the garden. He would always do it from behind; he'd follow me to the toilet and make me sit on his knee backwards and each time he would put his hand over my mouth to stop me from screaming out. Once he tried to put his penis in my mouth but I started to choke. He took it out and never tried that one again, I suppose he didn't want me to choke to death. He told me that while Mum was away I would be taking her place *the sick bastard*. He even kept me off school and told the others I was ill and had to stay in bed, *yeah that was true*. I did have to stay in bed, not mine but his. For six hours he raped me and in between he'd have a nap. A few times I tried to get away but he was a light sleeper so every time I moved he woke up and wanted to know where I was going, I told him the toilet and he would get out of bed and stand at the bedroom door just to make sure I go back into his room. Just before the others got home from school he told me to go to my room and get into bed and then he would get dressed and then go down stairs. As soon as Tess came home and came straight upstairs to get changed, I pretended to be asleep so she wouldn't ask any questions.

I started to have nightmares and wake up screaming. Tess just said "go back to sleep." He came in and asked if I wanted to stay with him, I said "No" he seemed to be okay with that. He would never force me into anything while all the others were in bed. The next day I knew I made him angry because I said no to him. He kept me off school again but this time he told them that I had a bad night and needed to sleep. I didn't get to sleep, he started all over again with me. It was different this time, because I'd upset him the previous night he said "You need a lesson on the right thing to say," which was yes. He just didn't have sex with me, he forced me to have anal sex. The pain was so bad I thought he'd split my back passage open. He then said "If you ever wake up with a nightmare again and say no I'll give you the same as you've just had." This was a punishment because I said no, *what a twisted evil bastard* . I went to bed each night lying awake wondering if he was coming in to get me, listening for the floor boards creaking and shaking with fear thinking if it wasn't me, would it be one of the others? Fear of going to bed was so over whelming every night I felt sick to my stomach. Eventually, tiredness would overcome me and I'd fall asleep. When I woke up with nightmares after that punishment I made sure I never screamed. But the bastard lied to me. Although I never screamed he still did it just as a reminder. I didn't need reminding the pain was enough the first time. My life went on like that for months. One day out of the blue, he told us we were going to see Mum. We hadn't seen her in at least eight or nine months. All I know it was such a very long time but we had to wait until the weekend. A few more days wouldn't make any difference, we've waited that long.

The school was really concerned about how things were at home because my school work had been affected, I was slipping behind in my subjects so I kept being called into the heads office. Apart from my work not being up to standard I was also skipping classes and eventually school. The teachers couldn't understand what was going on with me, they knew there was something wrong. I was always on form with my subjects. *God knows I wanted to tell them, but how could I?* The weekend was there and off we all went to see Mum. The smile on her face when she saw us, it was like the sun beaming down melting the winters snow. It was really good to see that smile and how we missed it. A mother's intuition told her something wasn't right, she said "Is everything okay?" We told her everything was fine. She looked at me with a look that said, "What's wrong?" I so much wanted to tell her the truth but I couldn't. It would have really hurt her. Just before we got on the train for Stoke, he told me that if I said anything no one would believe me and I would be put into care for being a liar. All I could do was keep smiling at Mum, but she knew it was a fake smile. The whole time we were there he never left my side. When we got home there was a letter from school waiting and by the look on his face you could tell he wasn't happy. What was in the letter and who was it about? He told Tess to take the kids to the park, I knew then it was about me. After they left he made sure they were out of sight and then locked the doors. I knew what was coming but I wasn't prepared for the beating he had in store for me. He took off his belt and made me bend over the arm of the sofa, I thought *I'd rather have a beating than anything else*. This time he used the buckle end of it. By the time he'd finished all of my back was one big bruise. The pain was agonising then he raped me again and again, then he said, "You will get the same punishment if you skip school again," and then he sent me to my room before the others got back from the park. When they got back Tess came up to see me and asked if I was alright. She could see I wasn't. I was on my stomach and when she saw the bruises she started crying and said, "You should try to do what he tells you and stop skipping school." If only she knew maybe she wouldn't have said that. I don't think she was crying for me, I think she was crying because it could have been her getting the beatings. After that day I got worse, I started to drink. *I nicked his precious whiskey.* I was trying to numb the pain, not just the physical pain but the psychological and emotional pain as well. I went to school smelling of the whiskey. *He didn't notice the level on his bottle going down.* The school rang him to come and get me they couldn't have me in school smelling of alcohol. I knew I'd be in for it when he got me home, *you would have thought by now I would have tried to do things different but I didn't.* All I thought about was numbing all the pain and anguish I was feeling. He never said a word on the way home from school. We walked through the back door this time, he didn't lock it, he told me to go and put my things away then come back into the kitchen. When I got back in there he a ring on the cooker lit. I thought he was going to make himself a cup of tea, *we didn't have an electric kettle back then.* He grabbed hold of my hand and put it so close to the ring it almost burnt me, he said to me, "Next time you steal my whiskey I'll burn your fucking fingers." He wasn't bothered about me going to school smelling of it, the fact was he wouldn't have enough left for himself. I said to myself, "*I hope the bastard chokes on it.*" As each day went by I kept hoping that someone would realise what was going on in our house. Because I was young I didn't think that the only way anyone would know was if I told someone. By now he had convinced me that if I said anything I'd be taken away because it was all my fault. This particular day I was tidying up around the house when I came across a letter from Mum, I knew the risk but I had to read it. She penned her concerns about us and told him if everything went alright she'd be up for early release and hopefully be home in just over a month. I could feel my heart racing with excitement, thinking I'd have just over a month to go and then my nightmares would end. Until then I would just have to carry on and try not to set him off. I really thought that everything he was doing was because I was bad, I was wrong. The beatings became less frequent but the sexual abuse continued whenever he could. He was getting more daring now; it didn't matter if everyone was in the house. He called me upstairs, the excuse being he needed help with moving something. When I got up there he'd put a unit on the landing so nobody could get past it. I thought he was getting the room ready for when Mum came home, how wrong was I? He raped me in his room, I knew then it wasn't going to stop until Mum came home. He made sure I kept doing what he wanted, he hung his belt on the back of the door and made sure I saw it to remind me of what I'd get if I didn't keep doing what he wanted me to. How much more could I take? I didn't know.

The month soon passed and Mum was released. He couldn't even be bothered to go and meet her at the station, he just sat in his chair waiting for her to walk through the front door.

When she did arrive home the first words out of his mouth to her was not, welcome but "Where have you been I was expecting you hours ago?" She probably thought she'd be better off back inside. I wouldn't have blamed her if she had turned around and walked out of the door. He was soon barking out his orders, "I want a cup of tea, I need something to eat." Mum ignored him while she was kissing and cuddling us in turn. When it came to my turn Mum gave me the knowing look, the look as if she knew there was something wrong and then she gave me one of her smiles as if to say, "I'm home now, everything's going to be alright." If only she knew the truth, nothing was ever going to be the same again and there was no taking back what he'd done. It was a case of moving forwards. Lew hadn't touched me in a while, *great I was now free or so I thought.* However I was still getting the beatings and so was Mum. He threatened her that if she ever disobeyed him she would suffer the consequences and he would make her have sex with him in front of us all. Mum didn't know if he would but she wasn't prepared to take that risk. *On reflection I think he would have.* She couldn't win with him and there was nowhere else to go. Even if there was he wouldn't have let her take us all with her. He didn't want us but he knew it would hurt Mum if she didn't see us.

He realised that while she was in prison. All she's done now is gone from one prison to another, Lew now being the warden.

One Sunday afternoon, while Mum was doing her ironing and listening to her music on the Radio, he called me upstairs, I looked at Mum as if to say, *"HELP!"* then I thought to myself, *don't be silly all that has stopped, he wouldn't do anything with Mum downstairs. How wrong was I?* As I went into my room, he was sat on my bed. He summoned me over, got up and closed the door. As he turned around he said, "Your Mum might be back, but she's not being the wife she's supposed to be and won't let me touch her so you will have to take her place again." He forced me on the bed and raped me. He said, "This is how it's going to be until the bitch has sex with me." Like a fool I believed him until one day when I got home from school and I heard noises coming from upstairs. There were no sign of the kids so I followed the noises and they were coming from Mum's room. I knocked on the door and heard him say "Come in," I didn't expect to see what I saw, Mum and Lew having sex. I turned and quickly walked away. I found Robert, Ann, Marie and Alex in the girl's room. They were all sat on the bed scared to move. Tess wasn't home from school yet and then it hit me. He'll leave me alone now, he never did. The more he got the more he wanted. I asked myself, "Did he want it that bad, bad enough to start on one of the others?" I hoped not. He forced Mum everyday to have sex with him, I could tell by the noises and he'd force me whenever he could. Some days he'd force me in the afternoons and Mum at night. I was never going to be free of him and that's how it was.

One day there was a knock at the door. He answered it and when he came in there was a man with him. He introduced him as his brother Andrew. He said this is your Uncle

Andrew. Uncle Andy had a kind face and was ever so nice; Lew told us that Andy would be staying with us for a while until he got a place of his own. Lew started to be more careful while his brother was around. He obviously didn't want him seeing what he was doing to me, but he was still verbally abusive to Mum saying "Come on fat bitch we need a drink." Andy didn't like the way his brother spoke to Mum and told him not to be so cruel. Lew told Andy to keep his nose out of things that didn't concern him, it was between him and her. *At last someone to protect us from the beatings.* Andy managed to find himself a job in a warehouse. Every week he'd come home and gave us treats, mainly sweeties. We all started to get used to all the fuss Uncle Andy was giving to us and we were beginning to be happy just like we used to be, even Mum had a smile seeing us so happy. I had just started to trust him, when I realised it was a mistake to. This particular day was no different from any other. Andy had gone out and Mum was watching some soap operas on the television. We weren't allowed to watch much tele, it was there mainly for him to watch his football and horse racing. The only time we could watch it was when he was out and Mum was watching the soaps. But now he was using Mum watching her soaps to his advantage. I was sat with her then, all of a sudden! he called me. I didn't want to go so I asked mum "Is there anything you need doing" she told me there wasn't anything and said, "Go and see what your Dad wants." I had no choice, I had to go upstairs. I hoped Andy would come home, but he didn't. When I got up stairs he was stood near the bathroom, he told me I'd left it dirty and needed it cleaning. *Any bloody excuse.* He did what he needed to do with me and then went into his room. He shouted down to Mum and told her I wasn't allowed out and had to stay in my room but tell the others they can go out if they want to. I have never seen five children run so fast out of the door. It didn't matter that they were only allowed in the garden, he took advantage of every situation. While they were out playing and Mum was watching tele he raped me again, he didn't notice Andy had come home but he soon did when he came into the room and caught Lew in the act with me. Andy stood by the door; I looked at him with pleading eyes asking him to help me! He just turned and walked away. *What type of man would do that?*

Because we didn't have enough bedrooms Alex and Robert had to share are room while Andy had Robert's room. That evening I was playing in my room when Andy called me into his room. He said he wanted to talk to me about what he'd seen earlier. *Yeah he wanted to talk alright,* as I sat on the bed he turned and put his hand on my knee then asked me how long Lew had been doing that to me. I looked at him; I didn't know what to say so I said nothing. I just sat there expressionless, how could I tell him it all started when Mum went to prison? Almost two years ago, he just looked at me and said, "Never mind" and then started to put his hand further up my leg. Somehow I found the strength to say no. I wasn't going to let him do the same as Lew. He said to me "If you put up a fight I will tell your Mum you tried to touch me." All I could think of was *here we go again.* My strength was short lived, would Mum believe him? I hoped not so I said, "Go on then, I'm not bothered," then he changed his mind. I wasn't prepared for what he said next, "Well if it's not you it'll have to be one of the others," he ran through their names, "Tess too old, Robert wrong sex, Marie too mouthy, looks like it'll have to be Ann," I said you can't do that she's only four, the baby of the family. He didn't leave me a choice; I had to let him touch me. I was surprised because that's all he did. I thought he was going to rape me just like his brother, he then sent me back to my room. I hoped that was it, but deep down I guess I knew it wasn't over with him. A few days later Lew had gone out drinking and Mum decided she wanted to go and visit Isobel to thank her for all she did and tried to do for us while she was away. She asked Andy if he wouldn't mind looking after us, of course he didn't mind. We could see Isobel's house from our front window so Andy was watching to make sure Mum was there, he then asked Tess if she'd watch the others while he came up to see if I was okay. As soon as he came into the room he couldn't wait to touch me, this time he was really rough, then he forced himself on me. It didn't matter what he did he was really rough and hard as he raped me. After he had finished, and before he left the room, he went, "**Shush,**" and then said, "This is to be our little secret, but if you do tell anyone, I will make sure you suffer." With not really knowing him that well I didn't know what he was capable of, I had to believe he was capable of anything and assume every chance he got he would rape me time and time again just like his brother did. Andy stopped looking for somewhere to live and kept telling Mum there was nothing suitable for him, this went on for months until one day when I got home from school there was a woman sat on the sofa next to Andy. She was small with long black hair, olive skinned, quite a pretty lady. I thought *well he's got himself a girlfriend; maybe he'll leave me alone.* How wrong was I? She wasn't his girlfriend, she was his wife. Apparently she had flown in from somewhere abroad to take him back home wherever home was, it could have been Outer Mongolia for all I cared. I just wanted him out of my life for good. With him out of the way I still had to contend with Lew and the school bullies.

One Saturday Lew had gone out and, on his return he had a dog in tow, a German shepherd. We were all excited and thought we had a pet, that poor dog was so frightened of us she cowered into a corner. We tried to stroke her but she tried to get further into the corner shaking with fear. Lew said "Leave her alone, by the time I get her trained you won't be able to touch her." We asked him what her name was, his reply shocked me, "She has no name and don't give her one, she'll be called by the name Dog." We didn't think that was right, all dogs need a name. So we decided to call her Maxine. When Lew wasn't around we kept calling her that so she would get used to it. It took about a month before Maxine started to trust us, but when he was around she was a nervous wreck and would find somewhere to hide away from him. It was hard for us to watch him being so cruel to her. If she didn't respond to his commands he would hit her hard across her nose with his newspaper or his belt. It only made Maxine worse, *the poor dog, God knows what happened to her before he got his hands on her,* I reckon he was carrying on from her previous owners.

One night in particular he'd gone out drinking. He was so drunk when he came in he could barely walk and made such a noise he could have woken the dead. Luckily enough most of us were heavy sleepers. I was already awake, I'd had another nightmare. I could hear Mum and Lew having words or rather Mum tried to speak to him and he shouted at her. Most of the conversation was muffled but I did hear some of it clearly especially the part when he said, "When I get that dammed dog trained, I'm going to get it to bite you." Deep down I knew Maxine would never do that, she was all over us when he wasn't about but she was still scared of him. I knew I'd be alright tonight, he had that much to drink he couldn't raise a doubt let alone anything else. The next day he was in the foulest of moods, probably the worst mood we'd ever seen him in and we'd seen him in a lot of them. No one was allowed to speak. He demanded a full English breakfast. Mum didn't have everything in needed for it, so he went into one calling her all the lazy bitches under the sun, a useless mother and then said to her, "The only thing you're good for is fucking and you're not much good at that. Mum had been out of prison for quite a while and was still trying to get on with things but Lew wasn't making it easy for her *he never did make things easy*. Anything and everything that went wrong was always mum's fault but his excuse this time was her not being here for twelve months. Then as usual she was a useless and unfit mother and they should have kept her where she belonged behind bars. I couldn't do anything to make Mum feel better only give her cuddles but she needed more than those. I wished the evil bastard was dead. At the age of thirteen I shouldn't have had thoughts like that but I think God would forgive me under the circumstances.

There was a knock at the front door and, low and behold, there was the police officer that originally arrested Mum for the theft from the old lady stood there. When Lew saw the officer, he started having a go at Mum asking her "What have you done now." Things got so bad the officer had to intervene and told Lew to step aside away from her. After things had calmed down a bit the officer apologised to Mum for everything she had been through, being arrested and going to prison. He told her that the old lady's son had taken the things Mum had been accused of and had been charged with the offence and perverting the course of justice as he gave a false statement. The statement he gave which my Mum was found guilty. We all cheered. We knew she was innocent. Lew heard all this and his face said it all he had nothing to throw at her now, the relief on mums face and at least those doubting Thomas's will know the truth now. The officer said "You should get a letter from the police commissioner exonerating you. I shouldn't be here telling you this but I think after all you've been through you deserve to be told straight away. The letter from the commissioner will be with you in a few days and I would appreciate it if nothing was said about me being here today. Thank you."

Mum agreed and thanked the officer for his courtesy.

CHAPTER 5
THE RESCUE

Lew's threats, bullying and abuse were rife, *nothing new there*. There wasn't a day that went by that he didn't threaten, bully or abuse us. He would find something to complain about and even the younger ones were now getting a taste of his tongue lashings as well as me, Tess and Robert. But now, Tess and Robert were getting the beatings as well. There was one day I especially remember. I got into a bit of trouble at school. The bullies (*even to this day I don't know the name of the ring leader*) told a teacher I'd turned the taps on and flooded the toilets. When the teacher asked me about it all I could do was look at her. I didn't have a clue what she was going on about, all I could do was look at her. She took my silence as a sign of guilt. She did no more than to send a letter home and addressed it to Lew. She had no idea what an evil, sadistic bastard he was how could she? When he received the letter he did no more than to pick up the broom and hit me full force straight across my back.

Through the tears I could see the look on Mum's face, a look of absolute shock horror. She came over to me and tried to comfort me. He told her to get away from me because he hadn't finished with me. For the first time mum found the strength and wouldn't move. She told him to get out, she said to him "You had no right doing that to her," he just gave her an evil grin. She knew it was pointless telling him to go, he didn't listen to her. She was right. *Yeah*, he left the room but he soon came back and this time he had the dog lead a chain. He stood in front of us and said to Mum "You either move or you will get it first," but Mum was standing her ground. *God love her.* Before he did anything, Mum had the chance to tell me to get out. I grabbed the others and, instead of running out of the front door I fled upstairs to the smallest of the bedrooms. *Only God knows how she managed to give me the chance to escape upstairs with the rest.* Somehow Mum managed to escape from him and made her way up to us. We could hear her running up the stairs with him running after her. We opened the door just wide enough for mum to squeeze through. We got all the furniture and put it behind the door so he couldn't get in. It wasn't long before he was banging and screaming at us to let him in and trying to open it; he was a man on a deadly mission, a man possessed. It went quiet for a while. We thought he'd gone then all of a sudden, he was back trying, a different tact. This time he spoke quietly and calmly to each of us, trying to get one of us to open the door. We all refused. We'd all had enough of his mood swings, his drinking and gambling, this was the last straw. He started again with his banging and verbal abuse. It was so bad you could see the fear in Mum's eyes and the little ones trying to hide in a corner just like Maxine did. Both Tess and I agreed that we needed help; we opened a window to see if anyone was about. The street was empty, it was like a ghost town. There was only one way of getting help and one of us had to do it. Whoever it was had to be quick. Tess said She was useless and there was no way of getting out, I was just about to agree with her, when it hit me. The room we were in was just above the front door and over the front door was a ledge. I didn't say anything to her, I just thought *they needed to be rescued from this ogre*. I looked at my family; there was no life in them, the fear in their eyes was just like the fear I saw in Maxine's eyes when he brought her home. I had to do something. I went up to Mum and said "I won't be long, I'm going for help." She tried stopping me but my mind was made up. I knew what would happen if he caught me, but that was a risk I was willing to take. I opened the window as wide as I could and lowered myself onto the ledge, that was the easy part. The hard part was jumping about six and a half feet without breaking my neck or being caught by him. Just before I jumped, I looked around Mum was standing at the window. I blew her a kiss and then went for it. I hit the ground with a thud, but managed to get up and run as fast as I could, around the corner and up the hill to the nearest phone box, I rang the police. I tried to explain to them what was going on but they couldn't understand me. Then I spotted Isobel and called her over and explained to her what had happened. She rang the police and they told her that they would send someone out and for me to go back. There was no way I was going back there until he was out of the house. I went as close as I dared to the house, close enough to see the police, but not near enough for him to spot me. I seemed to have been waiting for ages when all of a sudden a police car turned up. There was only one copper, what could he do? I waited and watched him knock on the door. Lew obviously answered it, I couldn't hear what was being said but then the copper returned to his car and started to drive off. He was headed in my direction so I managed to stop him and asked why he hadn't been arrested? He said to me, "there's nothing I can do. I can't intervene between a husband and wife, I can only do something if someone is attacked." *Back then it was classed as a domestic argument*. I then turned and lifted up my top and showed him the marks on my back. The copper wanted to know how I got them and I explained to him what Lew had done to me and Mum and where he could find her and my brothers and sisters. The bruising on my back was enough for him to radio for back up and an ambulance; he didn't know what they would be walking into or if there would be any casualties .Lew was arrested and Mum was taken to hospital to have her cuts and bruises photographed. The doctors wanted her to stay in for observation but she refused, she couldn't trust anyone now. I was seen by the police doctor who took photos of my back. He suggested I stayed in overnight but just like Mum I refused. After Lew was questioned he was charged and released on the condition that he didn't come anywhere near the house and any of us. If we saw him anywhere near, we had to tell Mum and she would have to inform the police. That put us all on edge, all we kept doing was looking out of the window. We knew the bastard wouldn't listen to the police, he was a law unto himself and he'd say anything so the police would let him go. He did come back and as usual full of drink, he thought that if he intimidated us enough Mum would drop the charges. He knocked on the door and started shouting through the letter box. Mum quickly rang the police but, while she was on the phone to them, he managed to climb through a window. The police arrived very quickly and re- arrested him. This time he wasn't released, he was kept in the police cells over the weekend. I think he appeared in court. Mum never spoke about it. All we knew is, after a while, she applied for a divorce.

It took a long time for us to realise that bastard was never coming back. We still kept looking at the door every time there was a knock on it. The little ones didn't understand and kept asking, "When's daddy coming home?" *I don't know what she told them*. It took Mum a lot courage to do what she did, divorcing him. She found it strange being on her own with us kids. She might as well have been before, he was no help. *He was as much use as a chocolate tea pot.* It took quite a long time but, eventually, we all started to relax Maxine started to be the playful happy dog she was when he wasn't around, now she can be out in the garden with us, running riot. We were all getting to be a lot happier. We wouldn't venture away from the house for a long time afterwards, and when I was walking to school I had to keep looking over my shoulders to make sure he wasn't following us. As far as I was aware he never did. Now we were all rescued from ogre. The sense of freedom was more than a relief for most of us. I was still having nightmares but Mum put it down to everything that had happened. Little did she know how true that was. She thought, sooner or later, I would be alright. She kept asking if I needed to talk but I never did. I kept everything locked up inside of me. What else could I do? Mum was starting to get the sparkle back in her eyes and, when we looked up at her, she gave us that smile; the smile that reminded us of Scotland and the way she used to be. I couldn't take that away from her now.

The school now knew what had been happening at home because the police had to go to them to find out if any of us had said anything to them about it. What could they tell them? Nothing. However, there was a lot the school had to say to me and yet, again I was called into the heads office. I couldn't understand why Tess a Robert weren't called in but things didn't seem to affect them, or their school work as much as it did mine. I was their main concern. The headmaster asked, "Why didn't you say anything?" He soon got his answer, "Why should I say anything to you when you can't even stop a bully from picking on me in school? She might have stopped in school but she still picked on me outside and you didn't do anything about that either." After

I said all that, I just got up and walked out of his office and straight out of the gates. As I was walking across the playground towards the gates I thought to myself, "*that told him*". He didn't phone Mum straight away; he thought I just needed time to myself to cool off. But when I hadn't returned by home time, he had to ring Mum to let her know what had happened. Mum started to worry; no one had any idea where I was. Neither had I. When I walked out of school, I just kept walking and lost all track of time. When I eventually returned home Mum asked me where I'd been. I couldn't tell her, I had no idea. I didn't think what she might have been going through, or what she was thinking. Was she thinking Lew had taken me? I don't know, maybe. Although he was out of our lives, he was still mentally tormenting me. I kept reliving what the sick bastard had done to me. There seemed no escape, but I had to try to find a way to deal with it. I still couldn't bring myself to tell anyone. I thought about ending my life, but apart from causing Mum more pain and sorrow, the bastard would have won. I wasn't going to give him the satisfaction of thinking he wasn't going to reported, not knowing if the police were going to turn up at his door to arrest him for being a paedophile. He was probably going through life still drinking and gambling and not knowing. Just the thought that he might be suffering was a little comforting. What did help was the bully. She still got me after school, but things had to change and I was the only one who could do that, no one else could. Was I strong enough? Could I do it without being physical? I had to think about it but it didn't matter what solution I came up with, the question was would it work? Being practical, I was only fooling myself. In reality the only way to deal with it was to fight fire with fire. That was the solution. Give her a taste of what she had done to me over the years. I decided to wait for her after school and, when she turned the corner, she was shocked to see me standing there. She did no more than to come straight to me with her followers in tow. They all started with the verbal abuse. I just stood there and let them get on with it. I said nothing. After they had finished mouthing off, I looked at the ringleader and said "It's about time me and you had it out properly." She started laughing. I continued, "So tell your mates this has nothing to do with them and to stay out of it." The bully, thinking she was big agreed and said to them, "This won't take long." Her mates formed a circle around us, they couldn't help themselves, they probably thought I'd try to run, how wrong were they? She walked over to me and punched me in the face. As she turned flexing her muscles she must have thought she was Mohamed Ali. I grabbed her hair and pulled her back to me and put her into a head lock. *I must have thought I was Big Daddy,* punching the living day lights out of her. As I was doing this, I noticed the crowd getting bigger. Word must have gotten out I'd taken on the school bully and, there was Tess behind everyone trying not to be seen. The headmaster must have heard the commotion and came out to see what was going on. He soon put a stop to it, shame really, I was enjoying myself. He kept me and her behind, wanting to know what was going on, I told him I acted in self defence because she hit me first. He found it hard to believe because of the state she was in, however, because it was after school and not on the premises, there wasn't a lot he could do about it. He told us both to go home. I had no problem with that I'd done what I'd set out to do and showed her enough was enough. When I got home, Tess was already there and was telling Mum that I'd been fighting. Mum asked me what was going on and I told her everything including the part where Tess actually started it when she told them about my clothes. Mum was not happy about it and was just about to say something when there was a knock at the door. When she answered it, there was a woman and a girl stood there with blood all over her face and a ripped shirt. The woman started shouting at Mum and accusing me of picking on her daughter. *Mum bless her,* just laughed at the woman which surprised her enough for her to keep her gob shut. Mum then called me to the door and asked me again, "What was going on" again I told her that for the past two years, I had been bullied and how it all started. The girl lowered her head; her mother was just about to call me a liar when she noticed the look on her daughter's face. She knew then that her daughter had lied to her. She made her apologise to me and the family for any hurt she'd caused. After that I never had any more trouble in school but Tess did. She asked me for help, where was she when I needed it? It's funny how the tables turn. I should have said, "No you sort it out yourself," but if I'd done that I wouldn't have been any better than her. I was better than that and my family comes first.

Life seemed to get better for us and we were happy again. My nightmares had finally subsided. I hadn't forgotten what Lew had done to me but I still couldn't tell Mum. She had finally got her life back together and started to go out meeting people. We had just found out Maxine was expecting so we had something to look forward to *the patter of tiny paws.* Months had passed since my fight and the puppies had arrived. Seven of the little darlings, three boys and four girls. Mum told us not to pick names for them because we had to re- home them when the time came. Money was still tight but I was at an age now where I could do a lot more to help. I got myself a paper round in the mornings and two babysitting jobs twice a week and in the summer months Tess, me and Robert also picked potatoes at the local farm. I earned seven pounds from delivering the news papers and six pounds from babysitting. Whatever I got from picking spuds, I would give Mum at least half of it. I also found a

Saturday job on the local market and, during the school holidays I'd work Tuesdays on there as well selling handbags. I would also give Mum half my wages from there. It was the least I could do after all those years of her struggling and still doing so. She kept refusing but I wore her down and she had to give in. I kept busy all year and enjoyed it; I didn't have much time to think about things. Life was going really well now and I never thought anything else could happen. But as the saying goes *don't speak too soon*.

One day, Tess and I were on our way home from school. In the distance we could see flashing blue lights and, as we got closer we could smell something burning. I said to Tess, "Those lights look very close to our house." As we turned the corner, to our surprise we saw a fire engine parked near to our house, there were six houses in a row so it could have been any of them. I didn't think for one minute it could have been ours, Mum was always so careful. As we got closer we couldn't believe our eyes it was our house. There was nothing left of it, just a shell. I couldn't see Mum anywhere. We started to panic and then a neighbour told us she was in another neighbour's house in a state of shock. *Who wouldn't be after having their house burned down?* Then I remembered Maxine and her pups. I asked one of the firemen about them and he said, "They've all been taken the vets to be checked over." I was so happy they had been rescued. We then ran to the neighbours where Mum was, she said, "We'll have to move to another house until this one has been made safe and fit for us to live in again," Luckily enough we didn't have to move too far away, only a little way up the street near to the local park. Mum was beside herself with worry. Not having a lot of money, how could she afford to replace everything that was destroyed? There was no way she had the money to replace anything. We went across to see the damage and, to see if there was any chance anything could be salvaged.

There wasn't anything. It had all been burnt to a crisp. We all thought that just maybe there would be something we could find. The disappointed look on Mums face, *bless her*. We all went back to the other house. There was nothing we could do or say to help Mum, all we could do was to give her a big cuddle like she did with us when we were upset. Then there was a knock at the door. I went to answer it with Mum close behind me and to our surprise Isobel was stood there, holding two dinner sets and behind her there was a line of people all carrying things that we might need. Then, a big van turned up. We didn't think anything of it until the driver and his mate opened the back doors. *Oh my God* we got one of the biggest surprises of our lives! The men started to unload beds, a cooker, a sofa, tables and chairs and a fridge. They put the items in the rooms where they needed to be. We couldn't work out how people knew. One of the neighbours told us that, while the firemen were putting out the fire, Isobel went knocking on people's doors asking for their help. *That's the second time over the years Isobel helped us, what a good friend.* All Mum could do was cry. She didn't know that there were so many people out there willing to help a complete stranger. The generosity of those people was truly amazing. Then the Sally Army turned up with blankets, sheets and a food parcel. We couldn't thank them enough for their generosity. Mum was still upset, although the material things had been replaced the things that meant so much to her couldn't be; her photos, all the memories in those pictures had been lost. The next day, one of the firemen came round to see if we were alright and to ask if there was anything he could do for us. There was nothing he could do but mum thanked him for his kindness and thoughtfulness. Just as he was about to leave, he handed her a box and when she opened it her face lit up and her smile was just like it always used to. The fireman had found Mum's photo album.

The majority of the photos were unscathed.

It was a fresh start now and new memories to be made, Mum rang the vets to find out how Maxine and the pups were doing. By the time she got off the phone she was in floods of tears, I heard her say, "How do I explain this to the kids after everything they've been through?"She called us all together and tried to talk to us but found I difficult. Eventually she told us Maxine wouldn't be coming back. We asked about the puppies. Some of them survived but because of the injuries they had it wouldn't have been fair to them. They were suffering so the best thing was to have them put to sleep. Maxine wasn't just our pet, she was part of our family, our friend and now she was gone. Mum kept wondering how the fire started. She was always careful when it came to electrical things. She always made sure everything was switched off and unplugged before she went out and, at bedtime. It was her ritual so how did this fire start? She convinced herself that it was arson and Lew had started it to get back at us all. A few weeks had passed and we found out that the fire was caused through an electrical fault.

Things weren't the same without Maxine. When we'd come in after being out we would call her, expecting to run up to us wagging her tail and jumping on us for her to be stroked. Then we remembered she wasn't there anymore. Mum found it just as hard. While we were at school and when Ann was having her afternoon nap, Maxine was company for Mum, now there was only solitude until we came home.

Mum had two fears. One was the fear of water and the other was enclosed spaces. The only thing I was aware of mum being fearful of was Lew. One day, I went to the bathroom not realising Mum was in the bath. She just asked if I was okay but I noticed she wasn't sat in the bath like you usually do, she was kneeling in it. I asked her "Why are you kneeling in it?" Her reply was I'm scared. Also she never closed and locked the door and the same goes for the toilet door. I also asked her about that but she would never give me a straight answer only, "I'm scared." As the years passed I wondered if it was something from her childhood or was it something that Lew had done to her? We never saw anything to confirm it but me and my siblings weren't always about, I had my suspicions but was I right? I don't know.

CHAPTER 6
THE RUNAWAY

After losing Maxine and the pups to the fire, life as it was had taken a backwards turn for me. I was depressed and went into a state of self loathing, blaming myself for everything that had happened over the years. Every time I looked into a mirror, instead of seeing a young girl crying out for help, all I could see was an ugly, fat excuse for a human being. Tess and Robert didn't help matters. They would call me names, "piggy, pissy pants and ugly." If only they knew, I don't think they would have been so cruel. They did it behind Mum's back so she never heard or saw them. But they were expected me to help them if someone was picking on them. They knew it didn't matter what they called me, I would always help them. I also had the added pressure of trying to catch up with my school work, I'd fallen behind on almost every subject. I thought about ending it all, but what would that achieve? More pain and suffering to my family so I decided that it wasn't worth it, they'd been through enough. I'd hit an all time low. I didn't know what to do to pick myself up or how to do it. I was young and didn't know who to turn to, if anyone at all. By now Marie and Alex had started on me.

They blamed me for Lew not coming back. They said "It's your fault dad isn't coming back. If you hadn't phoned the police, he would still be here." It took them twelve months to bring that up. Maybe it was because Mum was going out more and had a few male friends and they thought that just maybe one of them would end up being their new Dad. They couldn't see beyond themselves. It was what they wanted and nothing to do with Mum being happy. She did her best to keep the peace between us all but it was hard for her. As soon as one argument finished another one started. She still didn't know about the names I was being called, all she could see was normal, sibling banter. Mum told me I had to give up my paper round and babysitting jobs because I needed to concentrate on my school work. I hated giving them up. They were my escape for a few hours from everyone, now I'd be around them all the time.

In the end, everything got too much for me. I thought I would be better off if I wasn't around them anymore so I decided to go back to Scotland. I had thirty pounds saved from my jobs which I was going to use for Christmas presents, so I decided to use that for my trip. I worked out that if I used it on fares there wouldn't be enough left for food so I went to the schools library to find the best way to get there and wrote it all down. Just by pure luck, Lucy's parents invited me to spend the weekend with them; they were going on a day trip to the coast so Mum agreed I could go with them. *This was my chance*. I packed a few things I thought I needed, and then gave Mum a kiss on the cheek and left with her waving me off. As it happened I had to go the same way as I would have done if I was going to Lucy's. I had to walk around a few houses until I managed to get on to the road I thought I needed, then had to work out which way was North. I was trying to thumb lifts. Although I was scared I didn't think there were any other options. After about an hour, I managed to get my first lift. The driver was only going forty miles up the road but it was forty miles away from the torment I thought I was leaving behind me. That wasn't the case the torment of what Lew and Andy did to me wasn't that far behind me. The driver dropped me off and told me which road would be the best for me to get to my destination. Before he drove off, he also told me to stay on the B roads because they'd be a lot safer for me. Like the driver said I stayed on those roads but I had no idea which way to go. Despite looking on a map for the best route to take, it wasn't working out that way. I had written down most of the places I should have gone through but I never saw any of them. I seemed to be miles off route, I was lost and confused and wished I'd never started this adventure but I had to carry on there was no going back, back to those memories. I needed to make new ones and this was the start. All the new places I would see and the people I would meet, or so I thought. I continued on my journey, hitch hiking going through various places, Leamington Spa, Hinckley, and Birmingham. I decided to stay in Birmingham for a few days and have a good look around. I had no idea where I was going to sleep but I was sure I'd find somewhere, so I stuck my bag on my back and walked and walked and walked. I was starting to get tired and it was getting dark. I came across some flats with stairs on the outside so I went underneath them. It was cold and dark *but at least I'd be safe* I thought to myself. I could hear people coming and going, up and down the stairs and noises from within the area. I did manage to get a few hours sleep though but it wasn't enough, I had to find somewhere else or move on. With not knowing the area, it was difficult so I started making my way out of the town when I came across the famous Bullring shopping centre. I didn't think much of it. To me it was a dark dismal place but it could have been the way I was feeling which made everything seem that way. Being in the town had an advantage; no one knew me so there were no questions being asked and no lies to tell. I could be myself, whoever that was. It had been too long since I could do that. Somehow, I found a derelict shed on an allotment. It was ideal for what I needed and it was only going to be for a short while. It was quiet, maybe a little too quiet. As I settled down for the night and started to drift off to sleep something made me jump. It was just noises from outside. It could have been animals scurrying about, I don't know. The slightest of noises would awaken me but, in the end, tiredness caught up with me and I fell asleep. I was eventually woken up by a man poking me with a stick. He asked me what I was doing there and, as I tried to explain to him nothing would come out. I wasn't scared of him; there was something in the way he looked at me that said he wasn't going to hurt me. I tried again to explain what I was doing there. I assumed if I told him I was a runaway he would call the police so I told him my father had kicked me out because I was out of control and I was trying to get to the rest of my family in Scotland. He told me he believed me but I don't know if he did or not. He asked me if I was hungry and when was the last time I had eaten. I said, "I ate last night, I had a sandwich," and I showed him the sandwich wrapper. *Hell yes I was bloody starving.* He took me to a café not too far from where he lived. Being in a café surrounded by people I thought I'd be safe. After I'd eaten he wanted to know if I'd like to go back to his house to get cleaned up. He could see I was on edge but told me his wife would be there. I needed a change of clothes and a good wash so I said yes. When we got back to his house, he showed me to the bathroom and told me he was just going to see his wife. There was no lock on the on the door. I didn't think anything of it. He knew I was in there so he wouldn't come in, would he? I stripped down to my underwear and was having a good wash when the door opened. He stood there looking me up and down. I tried to reach for the towel to cover myself up but he got it before I could and then he closed the door then leaned against it. There was no way out, the window was too small. He came over to me, still looking me up and down and then he grabbed my arm and said, "you owe me for breakfast," I tried putting him off by saying "your wife may come in." It was then he said "She won't, she's bedridden." Then he raped me. When he'd finished with me he was taking me down stairs to make a drink. As we passed his bedroom I saw his wife asleep and her hands tied to the bed posts. I had to get out of there. He locked the front door when we came in so that was out of the question. However, I managed to find an open window. I climbed out of it as fast as I could. I was reliving my past. I thought Lew and Andy were the only ones that would do something like that, I was so naive didn't think there would be any more like them. I had to get away from here and back on the road again. I wasn't going to rest until I got as far away as possible from Birmingham. But I still had to get lifts from strangers. At this point, I almost went to the nearest police station so they could get me back home. I don't know why I didn't. I just knew I had to get out of that place. I didn't know at this time that the police were already looking for me.

As soon as I found the right, road I got a lift almost straight away. This one was going to Stafford. The driver tried talking to me but I stayed silent until he dropped me off and then I asked him how to get to Newcastle. He just pointed to the motorway. "That's not a B road," I said, he said, "It's the quickest way, walk to where the motorway says Stafford." I did that and just sat down and waited. It wasn't long before a lady in a van stopped and wanted to know if I needed a lift. I said, "I need to get to Newcastle," Totally forgetting there were two of them. She wanted to know which one,

"Newcastle upon Tyne," I said, she explained that she had a delivery to make but she was on her way up there herself. Her first stop was at Newcastle –Under – Lyme, however she had to drop me off before she got to where she was delivering. She wasn't supposed to carry passengers; it was against the company's rules, so she dropped me off at the corner of the road. I thought she was just saying that but I decided to wait anyway. She did come back for me. Her next stop was Bradford. Again I got out at the corner of the road and waited for her. Her final drop was Newcastle-upon-Tyne. We stopped to get something to eat; by now I was starving. She went to pay for mine but I said "no thank you, I'll pay for my own." I didn't have a lot of money left but I had enough for a drink and a sandwich with a little left over. After the last time I didn't trust anyone. She might have been a woman but I still didn't trust her. We were back on the road again and soon we reached her final destination. I thanked her for the lift and asked her, "Which is the best way to Carlisle?" She had a bemused look on her face but told me anyway. I was on my own again. I decided to stay in Newcastle for a while but this time I was going to be more careful to who I spoke to and where I went. While I was walking around, I found the ideal place to stay, a derelict house. There were other people in there all sat around in one room. I explained to them I only needed shelter for a few nights because I was on my way to Scotland. They had a meeting and agreed I could have the spare mattress for as long as I needed it. They said "You'll be safe here and no one will try anything because you're underage. Putting you up is one thing, but anything else is a no and that includes drinking alcohol." They were looking out for me, at least for the time being. I'd now be able to get a few decent night's sleep before I hit the road again. I stayed there three days and four nights. They really did look after me and made sure I had plenty to eat. There was one girl, not much older than I was and we seemed to have a lot in common. She started to tell me how her father beat her up but when any of the others walked by, she would quickly change the subject. I didn't get as far as to tell her my story. I didn't know if I really wanted to. One of the older squatters explained how things worked. Apparently, they only stayed in one place a short time then moved on before the police came to remove them. If the police came, things normally got out of hand and they would physically be moved from the property. So that the peace would be kept, they left before any of that could happen. The day arrived for them to be on their way and they asked me to go with them but I declined and thanked them for taking care of me. I needed to get back to Scotland, that's where I belonged. I walked to where I could get a lift and waited and waited for what seemed to be a lifetime before anyone stopped. Then, a lorry came past me. I thought *there goes another one* but this one stopped a little further down the road. As I walked towards it, I was expecting him to drive off. I walked around to his window and told him I was trying to get to Carlisle, he said, "I can take you half way." It was better than nothing. I ran around and climbed into his cab, *I was getting an expert at doing that.* We didn't talk much, he had one of those C.B radios and, as soon as he drove off he started a call on it. I knew nothing about those radios so I didn't ask about it, I guess I wasn't that interested in them. He dropped me off at a junction and told me to stay on this road then he drove off. I carried on walking; it wasn't long before the next lift came, another lorry. This one was going to Carlisle. That suited me just fine. I got on board and he also had one of those C.B radios. As soon as he drove off, he was straight on it. He gave out the same call as the other driver did, they talked in a sort of code which I didn't understand and this time I asked him about it but he said, "There's nothing to worry about." It would have been pointless pursuing it.

While I was busy running away from things, I totally forgot about Mum, I didn't think that what I was doing was hurting her. I'd been gone for just over a week. Mum must have been sat by the phone, expecting a call to say that I'd been found safe or worse. She was probably frantic and sick with worry, but all I could really think of was getting to Scotland. We had almost reached his destination when he stopped and said to me, "It would be best if you got out here because if I'm spotted with you in my cab I could lose my job." That was the last thing I wanted to be was responsible for, especially after he was kind enough to give me a lift, knowing what could have happened. As I got out of the cab I thanked him and then I asked him "which is the best way to Scotland?"

He replied, "The best road is that one over there," and pointed, "It will take you straight to Glasgow if that's any help." He was more help than he realised. By now, dusk had fallen and it wouldn't be too long before it went dark. I was getting hungry and there was nothing headed in that direction. I would have had to find somewhere to rest before doubling back to the road I needed. So I had to stay where I was. Then I decided to walk as far as I could before the darkness fell. I don't know how long I'd been walking before it crept up. There had been no traffic on the road. Then all of a sudden, I could see lights coming my way. I stopped in my tracks, hoping that they would stop for me. I couldn't have carried on much longer. As the lights got nearer to me, I could see it was a lorry. It stopped a little way down the road. I picked up my bag and headed towards it. I told the driver where I was heading and got into his cab. It was nice to sit down, my feet were throbbing. He also had a C.B radio. It was quiet, no one was talking so I guessed there wasn't many lorries out at night. The driver didn't say too much, he was singing along to the songs on the normal radio; songs from the sixties, songs that I loved so it didn't bother me if he spoke, I could just relax and close my eyes for a while. I must have fallen asleep because the next thing I knew, the driver was trying to wake me. We had reached Glasgow. As I got out I thanked him and asked, "Which is the best way to Edinburgh?" He wrote it down for me, and then drove off. It would be worthless trying to get any further so, with the last of my money, I was going to get a fish and chip supper and find somewhere to put my head down for the night. As I walked to the fish barI noticed a police car. I didn't think anything of it. I hadn't seen one in a long while and I never dreamt that they were parked there for any other reason than to get something to eat. As I was just about to go into the fish bar, one of the officers called out my name and, like an Idiot, I turned around. I wasn't expecting it so, because I was stupid, I got nabbed, taken to the nearest police station and put in a cell over night. I told them I was hungry so they sent out for fish and chips for me *at least I didn't have to pay for them*. There was one thing that puzzled me and still does to this day; how on earth did they know I was going to be at that fish bar at that time? After I had eaten they let me rest for the night, they thought after a good night's sleep I'd be more amenable to what they had to say. The next morning a police woman came to see me and wanted to know what I wanted for breakfast. She gave me a list.

On it was kippers, porridge, Scottish breakfast rolls or cereal and toast. She must have thought I was a pig when I asked for kippers, porridge and a roll. What I would have given for the taste of the old! I could feel my mouth start to water as I remembered the tastes. She came back with everything I had ordered and I sat and savoured every mouthful. After I'd finished the police woman came back to ask me. "Are you hurt? Is there anything you need to tell me?" I knew what she was getting at but she wasn't getting anywhere with me. If I had told her about the man in Birmingham then everything else would have come out and I wasn't ready for that yet. She also asked me about going home. With that one I looked at her and said, "I am home." I knew that's not what she meant and that's how it was for quite a few days. How could I leave all those mouth watering foods that I almost forgot about? And the smells that made all my senses come alive, now why would I want to leave again? That's what I told her, and she said, "If that is the case then you'll have to be put into temporary care because it's not suitable for you to stay here. The officer also said "I wasn't a criminal. To be honest you would be better off going back home because the only place that could take you at fourteen would be a children's home, no foster family would take on a teenager with problems." I didn't have much of a choice but to go home. I had to tell them where I was from. As it was late they kept me in one more night which gave them time to phone whoever they needed to and also contact Mum. They let me speak to her. It was the first time in over two weeks since I last saw or spoke to her. She couldn't say anything, all she could do was cry and thank God I was safe. After she managed to compose herself she told me that they'd moved back into the old house. *I was screaming in my head, "No mum, please not that house!."* I couldn't settle that night. All that kept going through my mind was that house and what had happened to me in it. The next morning, I was put on the train. They told me I needed to change at Birmingham. What they didn't tell me was that at each station, the Station Master would be checking to make sure I was still on the train. I had no intention of going anywhere but home; I needed to see my family but I wasn't prepared for going back to the old house where it all begun. As the train came to a halt at Birmingham, the Station Master came and got me. He had to wait with me for about an hour before I boarded the next train for the last leg of my journey home. I couldn't really describe how I was feeling at this point. I suppose I had mixed feelings, happy to be seeing Mum again and apprehensive because of what happened to me there. We soon arrived at my destination and, as the train was pulling into the station, I looked out of the window. I could see Mum waiting there with a strange man. When I got off the train, I'd never seen Mum move so fast. She almost knocked over some of the passengers on the platform. The man I saw never moved. I wasn't quite sure if they were together or not. As mum got nearer to me I could hear her say at the top of her voice, "Praise the Lord for her safe return." It was quite embarrassing really, what would people think of her? But when I thought about it, it really didn't matter what people thought; that was my Mum and she was pleased to see me; if she wanted to shout at the top of her voice then she could. Before I knew, it she was right in front of me. My eyes were still fixated on this man, even when mum grabbed me and gave me the biggest bear hug ever. I couldn't quite get my breath but I wasn't going to tell her to let go. She was crying so much I thought she was going to flood the station. We must have been stood there a good five minutes, when she eventually let go she started talking to me but I didn't hear a word she said. I asked her, "Who is that man?"I was shocked by her reply, "My boyfriend, we've been seeing each other for six months." None of us had any idea she was courting Mum didn't tell us because she wanted to make sure he was nothing like Lew. I asked her "how could you trust another man?" She told me he was different. "All men are the same," I said to her. "What happened to you over the last two weeks to make you so cynical?" Mum asked. "Nothing, but after Lew how could you, I can't see how things will be different with him." Mum then said, "His name is Henry and he's been brought up to respect women," "so was Lew wasn't he?" I replied, Mum couldn't answer that one, she just looked at me and then at Henry. I think at this point she realised it was going to be an uphill struggle to convince me that he was different, and she was right. I had my reasons but, unfortunately Mum had no idea what they were and I still couldn't tell her. I could see he made her happy, so I waited and watched for the slightest signs.

At the house things were different. It was like a new one; a different smell but the memories were still the same. No matter where I looked, all I could see was Lew. In the laundry room where Maxine used to sleep, I could see her and the pups. It seemed I was the only one who remembered what it was like. If any of the others did they never said anything. Things were never talked about so I tried to carry on as normally as I possibly could. I was finding it very hard so I tried to spend as much time away from that house as I could. I was outside this particular day when I saw a lad I'd never seen before sat on a wall. He started to speak to me. I told him I didn't want to talk but he just wouldn't leave me alone. I told him again, "I don't want to talk to you," in the hopes he'd go away. He just sat there in silence. I wanted to know what game he was playing, "I'm not playing a game, I just want to get to know you and, if I have to sit like this every time I see you, then so be it because sooner or later you'll speak to me." He was very sure of himself. I wasn't sure if I liked his body language and I wondered was it a front or was it him? I'd been hurt so many times in the past I couldn't even trust a lad. I asked him "how old are you?" He told me he was eighteen, almost three years older than I was. I wasn't quite fifteen, so what did an eighteen year old boy want with a young girl my age? I didn't get his name, but I wasn't that bothered.

I longed to be away from here. I still didn't feel as though I belonged. What could I do? Put up with it or do something about it? The nightmares returned, every night the same one. Lew and Andy, was creeping into my room and raping me. Some nights I would wake up Screaming with sweat pouring off me like a waterfall. Mum was getting concerned and told Henry about the nightmares I was having. While I was back home Henry never stayed the night. I don't know if he did before my return, no one ever said and I didn't ask. Maybe I should have done but at the end of the day, it was none of my business, I just didn't want Mum to get hurt again. The nightmares continued for weeks until, one day, I'd had enough and decided to get away. I needed to get back to Newcastle-upon-Tyne in the hopes of finding the squatters that took care of me last time. I packed a few things and walked out of the door. I knew it would hurt Mum and I hoped one day she would understand. This time, I wasn't going to hitchhike, I had a few quid saved up from my pocket money so I made my way to the train station and got myself a platform ticket and waited. The train to Birmingham pulled up and I thought it was the one I needed so I just got on it. As it was pulling out of the station I noticed the inspector was on his way round checking the tickets so I quickly went to hide in the toilet until he had passed. When he'd passed, I went to find myself a seat. I was on edge in case the inspector came back. If he'd caught me without a ticket he would have phoned the police and have me arrested for fare dodging. I had to find somewhere to hide. I noticed at one of the stops that people were putting bikes and suitcases on further down the carriages so I got off and headed towards where they were putting them on. Unfortunately there was a bloody guard in there. I realised the inspector didn't come this far down so I managed to sneak on without the guard seeing me while his back was turned, sorting out all he luggage and bikes. I hid behind a large trunk that was already in there on the other side of the carriage. The chances of getting caught were high but, in a way, it made it all the more exciting. We finally reached Birmingham and I got off without being caught, *phew, how lucky was I?* There was a long wait before the next train and it was risky for me to stay on the platform. The ride on the train was free but at the end of the day, I stole. Yes I stole from the railway. There was no guard on the gate so I managed to leave the station. It was then I remembered I didn't have any money left, I was stuck with nowhere to go and no more money. Had I made a mistake running away again? Or would I have been better staying, facing my demons and telling Mum what had happened when Lew was still around? No! I couldn't do that. I still blamed myself for letting it happen to me. I should have done more and said no more. Deep down I knew it wasn't my fault but I couldn't stop blaming myself. I was at a crossroads in my young life, not knowing which way to turn. I even hoped that one day someone would kill me to release my pain.

I walked around for a while then I came across a group of Rastafarians. I tried to avoid them but one of them came over to me and started to speak to me. I couldn't understand a bloody word he was saying and I told him so. I remembered what I had been told about what not to say to certain people, certain people being the negro community. I took a few steps back, getting ready to make a run for it but he just looked at me and said, "Why is there so much pain in your eyes? Someone must have really hurt you." I looked at him in disbelief. How could he tell I'd been hurt? By now I was feeling sick with hunger and, with no money, I wasn't sure what I was going to do next. I think he realised that and asked me if I was hungry. I just nodded, "Come with me," he said I asked him, "Where to?" He replied "to my house." I shook my head. For some reason I felt I could trust him and told him about the man last time I was here, then I said to him, " I will never make that mistake again." He told me his wife and children were there but I didn't believe him. He told me to wait where I was. I wasn't sure what for and, before I could say anything he disappeared. A few minutes later he came back with a woman and introduced her as his wife. I was still very unsure but I was so hungry I decided to take the risk. As it happened *thank God* he was telling the truth; it was his wife and he had three kids as well, two girls and a boy, I started to feel a little relaxed now. His wife got hold of my hand and guided me into the kitchen where the rest of their family was gathered. His mother and father told me their names but because of their accents, I couldn't understand a word they said either. Well, not everything that was said, to be honest all I was interested in at that moment in time was the food on the table. One of the girls took me to sit near to her at the table. I was in a right mess so I asked if I could clean myself up and his mother said, " In the bathroom." My face when she said that, the look of horror. She told me she'd take me and wait outside. It was obvious that the man must have explained to her what had happened to me last time. The relief showed on my face when she offered to wait outside the bathroom. I quickly cleaned myself up and was soon sat back at the table. I had never seen so much food on a table before! Various meat and fish dishes and many other dishes I'd never seen before but I didn't care. I was willing to try anything and everything as long as I filled my belly! I must have been there about three hours when I told them I'd have to leave. I needed to find somewhere to put my head down for the night but his mother asked me, "Where are you going to stay?" I'd had enough of lying so I told them the truth, "I don't know." His wife spoke to me next and told me that I would be welcome to stay with them for as long as I needed to. However, I would have to help around the house. I didn't have a problem with that. At least I'd have a roof over my head and regular meals. I did more than to help around the house; I took the kids to the park and played with them. I didn't mind they were lovely kids and ever so polite. I'd been staying with them for almost two weeks when we all went to the park for a picnic. While we were there I noticed some policemen kept looking at me. I knew what was going to happen and that I had to get away from the family. I didn't want them involved anymore than they already were. I tried to quickly explain to them and I got up and walked away. I got so far and then I started to run. I wasn't very fast on my feet and it wasn't long before the policemen caught me. As they'd gotten hold of me, I saw the man coming towards us. I had to stop him somehow so I shook my head and he seemed to understand and walked straight past us. For all the people who had told me to be careful of coloured people as I was growing up, saying that they were no good and took drugs and they get you into them, *let me tell you. The people that took me in were the nicest, kindest people I have ever met in my short life and didn't take drugs.* Staying with these people I learnt one thing; never judge a book by its cover. As the police were taking me to their car, we walked past the family and all I could see were sad faces and tears in their eyes and there wasn't anything I could do to comfort them.

I was taken to the local police station. One of the officers asked me why I'd run away. Like last time all he got was my silence. He told me they were making arrangements for me to go home and I asked, "What arrangements?" If it was by train then I could escape again. I wasn't that lucky. This time they were driving me home, back to the nightmares, Mum busy with her new man and the rest of them who didn't seem to understand what I was feeling, even though they saw what went on with Lew. But how much though? I was unsure about that. The car pulled up at the front of the station, I was escorted out and put into it. It was going to be one hell of a long drive back. I kept thinking of ways to escape again but it was futile, there was no way I could escape from this situation. I was hoping they would take me to my local police station but that was hope dashed; they took me straight home. As we pulled up, Mum was looking out of the window for us and Henry was standing next to her. As the officer opened the car door for me to get out I just sat there in the back seat looking at Mum. I had done it again; caused her pain and heartbreak. I just didn't think how much pain and hurt I had caused her. Some people may have thought I was self centred and just thinking of myself. Maybe I was, but all I could see was the family seemed to be getting on with their lives and forgetting what that tyrant had done to us, a family that was so close and was now so far apart. I couldn't forget. Maybe I should have tried but I didn't want to.

The young man I saw sat on the wall that day found out I was back. I didn't know Mum knew him but she told me his name is Alan. She told me he came round everyday to see if I was back, *that was nice of him*. She also told me that his aunty lived at the top of the road. She didn't know her really only to say hello to in passing. Alan became a regular visitor while I was at home and Mum hoped, with him coming round every day, it would keep me here, but only time would tell. Alan and I became good friends and that's how I wanted it to stay. I didn't know if I'd ever be ready for any kind of relationship or even having any children of my own. Andy and Lew destroyed all that.

Alan and I spent a lot of time together so Mum decided we were in a relationship and told the world and his wife. I should have spoken out and said to her, "We are not in a relationship we are just good friends," But the look on

Mum's face said it all. The look of disappointment, thinking I was going to settle down. I was still having the nightmares and now Alan was in one of them. In this particular nightmare, Alan walked in and caught Lew raping me. It looked as if he was going to join in but instead he pulled Lew off me and beat seven shades of shit out of him. Maybe, if it had really happened like that then I wouldn't have had so many demons controlling my sleep. By now Henry started to stay over a couple of nights a week. One night, when he was there, I woke up screaming. Henry came in to see if I was alright but when I saw him I just froze on the spot. I thought he was the same as Lew, and then I caught sight of Mum at the door, and I knew then he meant me no harm. The following morning Mum asked me, "Why did I react the way you did last night?" I couldn't answer straight away; I looked at the floor until I thought of something. She asked me again so I told her "I'm not used to him checking up on me I'm only used to you. It was a bit of a shock to see him stood there." Luckily enough she believed me and said no more about it.

Life continued as before; I was trying to be as normal as I possibly could and Alan keeping me distracted for a while. But I started to get itchy feet. It wouldn't be long before I was off again but this time but I knew they would expect me to go North again so I thought I'd fool them and change direction. I decided to go to London. A lot more people, a much bigger place and a lot more easier to hide in. I packed a few things in a different bag to the one that I normally used on my travels and as I walked out of the door, I told Mum I was going to the shop which was in the opposite direction to where I needed to go. As I got to the end of the street, I turned left instead of right and went down the hill, *which way now?* I walked in the direction as if I was going to school and headed towards Oxford. I'd work it out as I went along. I had no idea if I would end up in London or not, all I knew is that I had to head South. I reached Oxford with no problem and, while I was waiting for another lift, I met a girl who was also hitchhiking. She told me she was on her way to Portsmouth and like me she was also running away. She introduced herself as Kaz. I don't know if that was her real name or not and I wasn't really that bothered. However, she asked me if I wanted to go with her so we didn't have to travel on our own. *What a good idea, another female. We should be safer travelling together rather than on our own, and what harm could she cause* I thought. We managed to get a lift as far as Basingstoke. We had to go through Newbury first but, as soon as we were through there, we knew we were well on our way. We travelled through a lot of other places and lots of countryside. I didn't realise how beautiful and green our country was. We passed fields of rapeseed plants. The yellow of those plants was like a sea of sunshine, what a beautiful sight. The driver dropped us off just outside of Basingstoke and told us to head for Winchester. Luckily enough there were signs. We stood at the side of the road near to the sign post pointing in the direction of Winchester and, while we were waiting we got to know each other a little better. Like me, she didn't tell the whole story just what she wanted me to know. Then a car pulled up and asked us where we were going. Kaz told him Portsmouth. The driver told us that he could only take us so far because he was only going to Havant. We had no idea where that was but we said yes anyway. We travelled through Winchester and along the edge of Southampton and, after we arrived at Havant, we noticed a sign for Portsmouth. We thanked the driver for the lift and then we started walking and thumbing it again. It wasn't long before we got our final lift and before we knew it we were in Portsmouth. All we had to do was to find the sea front because Kaz was going to see her boyfriend who happened to be a sailor based there. We didn't know the part we needed was South Sea but we soon found out after asking someone. We made our way to the sea front. It had been a very long time since I'd seen the sea and I couldn't wait to put my feet into the water. When we found the area that we needed, it was different to how I remembered it. Kaz said, "I've got to go and find the naval base where my boyfriend is based." She said I could either go with her or stay where I was. I told her it was her time and I'd wait for her, so off she went. All I could do was to keep looking at the sea thinking and trying to remember how it was in Scotland with the sandy beaches and rock pools. This one was all pebbles with no rock pools. The sea was still the sea, it didn't matter what area you were, it was all the same. I picked up my bags and walked down to the water's edge. I took off my shoes and socks, rolled up my trouser legs and went in for a paddle. I began to feel quite queasy. I thought it was a touch of sea sickness *but what did I know?* After a while I walked back to where Kaz left me just in case she'd come back. I'd been waiting close on two hours before I spotted her walking really slowly, as if she was dragging her feet behind her. As she got closer I noticed her eyes were red as though she'd been crying. When I asked her what was wrong *I wished I hadn't* the floodgates opened and there was no way of stopping her. After quite a while, she eventually stopped and told me she'd seen her boyfriend Paul and all he could say was, "You shouldn't have followed me here, I've met someone else, go back home." *Talk about a kick in the teeth.* That's what she was going to do, there was nothing keeping her here now. I persuaded her to stay a few days longer in case Paul changed his mind. It was more like I didn't want to be left on my own here and I wasn't feeling too well either. We gathered up our belongings and went to find somewhere to bunk down for the night.

We seemed to be walking for ages before I spotted a bridge.

We headed straight for it, we were tired and really needed to sit down for a while. You could tell it had been used before because of all the cardboard that was under there, but we didn't know if it was still occupied. We took a chance and used some of the cardboard to sit on. We were both hungry *nothing new there*. A short distance away was a fish bar so Kaz went off to get us something to eat. *I didn't think she had any money*. When she came back, she had a couple of sausages and a bag of chips. I asked her where she got the money from she said it didn't matter and to eat up. It was now getting dark and we still didn't have anywhere to stay so we had stay put and hope we didn't have anyone's squat. This was the first time that Kaz had run away and she had no idea of what to do. Nor did I really but I did remember seeing some other shelters like this on my previous travels. I gathered as much cardboard as I could and tried to show her how to keep warm. I put some of the cardboard on the floor and the rest we made into one big box so we were able to crawl inside it, with our bags as pillows and our coats as blankets, we soon got warm and fell asleep. I wasn't asleep for long when woke up feel still feeling queasy and had no idea what was causing it. Kaz woke up and said she didn't have a good night. I had to laugh to myself she had a better night than I did! It was pointless saying anything to her. It was early, there was hardly anyone about so we got a change of clothes and went to the public toilets to get washed and changed *and of course to use the toilet*. After we'd done that, Kaz told me to take our things back to the bridge and she would get something for our breakfast. I was still trying to work out where the money was coming from, was it worth asking her? I didn't think she'd tell me so I didn't bother asking. She went off towards the town and I went back to the bridge but when I got back there I couldn't find any of our things. I looked outside. There was no one about so all I could do was wait until she came back. If she did then I know our things had been stolen, *who would do something like that.?* After a while she appeared from nowhere with a bag of shopping. She'd got us bread, milk and a few other things, enough to last the day. I kept thinking *where on earth she is getting the money from or was she shop lifting?* Then I remembered the sausage and chips she couldn't shop lift those, what the hell was she up to? She didn't seemed surprised when I told her about our things. It wasn't the reaction I would have expected; it was like she already knew. She said, "That's what happens when things are left out," how would she know if it was her first time sleeping rough? I had my suspicions but nothing I could prove. Nothing was adding up or making sense. Just like a bolt out of the blue she then told me she was going home. Something didn't feel right so, this time, I didn't try to stop her. I didn't need her, I'd managed before on my own and I was sure as hell could do it again. It was the company I wanted, but what the hell? She walked away and didn't even look back. I thought that was quite strange, then she walked into the arms of a sailor. Was that her boyfriend or was it someone else? I would never know.

I was on my own with barely any clothes and what I had needed washing. I had a bag of food which would probably only last a couple of days at best. Things were going to be different now; no money, only the clothes on my back and a few that needed washing. I had to find somewhere to wash them. A laundrette was out of the question, however, it was still early and there wasn't many people about so I took them to the sea. I took off my trousers and my top so they didn't get wet while I was washing the rest of my clothes. I got some funny looks from passersby but I didn't care and wasn't bothered what they thought. I decided to stay under the bridge for a few more weeks. It was ideal with it being close to the toilets and sea. I still didn't have any food and was still feeling sick but I put it down to lack of food. Every day I would walk into town for something to do, mainly window shop. I tried begging but barely got enough to buy a sandwich and a bag of chips. I got so hungry I ended up in the local supermarket and walked around for a while and, before I realised what I was doing, I was outside with biscuits, cakes, bread, milk and a few other items in my bag. I should have taken them back but hunger got the better of me. I ran back to the bridge as fast as my legs would carry me and then I realised that I'd committed my second criminal offence, I never thought for one minute I would commit another one after jumping the train.

I was starting to put weight on; I couldn't understand why I was hardly eating anything so I really should have been losing it and, by the end of the third week, I started to get sever stomach pains. They were that bad I had to find a hospital. I needed to know what was wrong with me and by now I gathered it wasn't lack of food. I headed off towards the town again and asked someone, "Where is the hospital please?" I was told there were three, Queen Alexandra on the other side of town, St Mary's and St James which were close to each other. I didn't know which one I needed, *but surely the hospitals were much the same?* The first I came to was St Mary's and by this time I was doubled up in pain. A nurse quickly put me into a room and I told her what the problem was, "A doctor will be in to see you as soon as he could," she said. She needed to check me over and wanted to know a few details like my name, address and age, I gave her false information. I can't remember those details I was in too much pain, then she asked me "is there any possibility you're expecting?"I said, "Expecting what?" then the penny dropped. I realised she meant pregnant, "No way on earth," I told her. She then wanted me to give her a water sample so off I went to the toilet. While I was in the toilet, the nurse went to get a portable scan machine and when I came back and saw it I wanted to know what it was for. She told me that the water sample indicated I was pregnant and she needed to check with the machine. I lay on the bed hoping it was a mistake. It wasn't. She wanted to know if I'd like to phone the father but what could I say? It was too much of a shock. I couldn't take it all in so I said, "No, he's no longer around." I was in early labour and needed to be transferred to the Queen Alexandra where they had the appropriate equipment for premature births. St Mary's was basically for A&E so all they could do there was give me an injection to try to stop the labour, but they weren't sure if that would do the trick. When I arrived at the Queen Alexandra, the doctors rushed with the midwives and nurses to try to stop the labour but whatever they did didn't work. I eventually gave birth to a girl weighing less than a bag of sugar. She was rushed to the special care unit. By the time I got to see her she was covered in tubes and was connected to various machines. I sat staring at her, trying to work out how it happened. I didn't have a boyfriend and Alan was just a good friend. The nurse was talking to me but I was so deep in thought didn't hear a word she was saying to me. When I realised she was speaking I asked her to repeat what she'd said. She said, "The chances of your baby surviving are slim, have you got a name for her yet?" I named her Charlotte. They called the priest so she could be christened. Charlotte only lived for eight hours. I was devastated. Then it dawned on me who the father was; it was that bastard who raped me in Birmingham. Maybe it was for the best it, wasn't the poor child's fault. I asked myself could I have brought a baby up knowing a rapist got me pregnant and knowing he was the baby's father? I don't know I did know if I wanted children when the time was right. Unfortunately, I couldn't afford a funeral for her; my poor baby was buried in an unmarked grave, all who were present were the vicar and myself. My angel deserved better but what could I do? I had only just turned fifteen, on my own and had no one to turn to. As I walked away, looking back with tears streaming down my face thinking I was dreaming, I saw the two bunches of flowers where she lay told me I wasn't. How could I have not known? No one could answer that. I walked around in a daze, not knowing what to do or where to go and how to replace what I had lost. That man had a lot to answer for. My life had already been ruined once before and now he ruined it again. Before I knew it, I was back at the bridge lying down under my boxes. I cried so much I fell asleep. I woke up after a couple of hours hearing a baby cry but it was just my mind playing tricks on me. I just lay there for hours until I fell asleep again. When I eventually woke up I was different, I seemed to be in self destruct mode. Every shop I walked into, I walked out with something. I didn't care if I was caught or not. I'd been living on the streets for about three and a half months by now and I learnt the best way to survive was to move around and not stay in one place for too long. I moved to a disused subway. I'd been watching to see how many people used it and no one ever did so all I needed was some more boxes. Instead of moving the ones under the bridge, I went behind the shops. They usually threw boxes and other things out there. I managed to find what I needed and much more; there was a bag of stuff that was thrown out by a charity shop. Apparently if they can't sell it they throw it out. In this bag was quite a few old blankets so I thought *if they don't want them well I do.* I took the whole bag with me; at least they'd keep me a lot warmer than the boxes. I had to make sure no one else would take them. Although no one else used the subway I couldn't be too careful and there was nowhere else to put them. I couldn't carry them around with me all day so I decided to go back to the bridge. I was better off there. I was getting to know some of the passersby. Although we never had any conversations they would always wave to me and say, "hello," the same time every morning and evening. Because they were regular I got to know what the time was. Back at the bridge, I disposed of the old cardboard and put fresh down. I folded a few of blankets in half and put them on top of the newly laid cardboard, then I made pillows out of some of them and the rest I used to cover me. I had made my little cardboard hut so comfortable that, once inside it, I didn't want to leave. But I had to. I needed food. What I wasn't aware of was that a girl about my age or there a bouts was watching my comings and goings me from her bedroom window. One day while I was out she left me a note with some food and clothes. The note read.

Dear Street Girl

I have been watching you for a while and you don't seem to have any friends I would like to be your friend as I don't have any myself and I get bullied at school.

You look so sad, just like me

Your friend,

Sophie

As I read the note I could understand where she was coming from but how could I be her friend? I had my own problems to overcome, how could I help her? I turned and looked around. I couldn't see how she could see me; all I could see was so many buildings which I assumed were hotels and B&B's. I couldn't tell if that's what they were as they had no signs outside or in the windows. For all I knew they could have been residential properties. After a good night's sleep, I set off walking past all these buildings to see if Sophie was looking out of any of the windows. I didn't see anyone so the only other option was to knock on all the doors and there was no hope in hell I was going to do that. When I returned there was another note.

Hi Street Girl

I know you've been walking up and down.

I take it you were trying to find me, When the time comes, we will meet. Until then......

The letter finished abruptly, I had no idea what she was trying to say. So I decided to leave her one.

Hi Sophie,

You say you want to be friends, but how can we when I don't know who you are and we've never met?

What were you trying to say in your last note?

You never signed it

Street Girl

Because we had never met I wasn't prepared to give her my name. She could have been anyone, it could have been a man posing as a girl, who knows? I didn't like the idea of her being able to see me. As far as I was concerned, she had the advantage over me. She wanted to be my friend but how can I be friends with a ghost? Until we actually meet that's all she was a ghost. The letters were going back and forth all week. Then one day on my return to my abode, I noticed a woman and a girl sitting on the grass verge which was highly unusual. No one ever sat on the grass near to the bridge or anywhere in the vicinity. This made me feel uneasy so I went through the other end of it. As I got near to my spot, the woman started to walk up to me. She wanted to know if I was Street Girl, I said, "Yes I am." It didn't take a P.H.D to work out the girl was Sophie and the woman her mother. I asked her why did she want to know? The woman told me that she had found the letters I'd written to her daughter. I told her I was just replying to the notes Sophie had left me and then I showed them to her, I said to her, "I was always brought up to respect people, and it was rude not to reply to letters or notes." I must admit, I found her notes very strange and the contents of them even stranger.

Sophie's Mum and I had a long chat and it was evident to me that she was an overprotective mother. She also wanted to know why I was on the streets. Without being rude I said to her, "Ask no questions get told no lies." I didn't want to tell her the truth and I didn't want to lie to her either. The fact of the matter was I didn't want to tell her at all. She was a stranger and I didn't think I could trust her. Sophie became a regular visitor after that day and we would sit and talk about anything. She would only stay a couple of hours then she'd have to go home. I asked why she wasn't at school; she came back with the same reply I had given to her mother. "Ask no questions get told no lies." I didn't think she'd heard me say that. She kept asking me to go back to her place but I would always refuse. After meeting her Mum the only way I'd go there was if her Mum asked me to. There was something about her mother that said it was a no go unless she said it was okay. Eventually her mother asked me round for my dinner. I couldn't go there looking like a tramp. After Sophie left, I had a walk into town and around the back of the shops again. They were just closing so I had to wait a little while for the staff to leave. I noticed a woman going around to the back of the charity shop carrying a few bags. I was hoping and praying none of the staff had noticed her and took the bags into the shop. I was still hanging about for quite a while after they had closed to make sure there were no people about. I did a lot of hanging about so they didn't think anything of it. The darkness was approaching and there were dribs and drabs of people on the streets but I decided to take a chance and go to the rear of the shops, hoping no one would see me. I found the bags the lady had left, *phew that was lucky they didn't see her taking them round to the rear of the shop and come out for them.* I grabbed hold of them and went to a side of a skip and had a good rummage. As I was rummaging through them I came across a pair of jeans that looked quite familiar. They looked like the pair I had stolen but that could have been a coincidence. The more I looked the more items in there looked like mine. I gathered the bags up and took them back to my cardboard abode to have a proper look. It was getting to be less of a coincidence, they looked exactly like the ones that were taken. I began to wonder if Kaz had stolen them and sold them or someone else had nicked them. I'd never know. I went through them with a fine tooth comb to see if there was anything to indicate they were originally mine but I couldn't see anything. The woman was kind enough to wash and iron them *how lucky for m.,* It was getting late so I called it a night and tried to get some sleep but I couldn't settle. All that was going around in my head was the clothes and how similar they were to the ones I had. I couldn't go to the police. Even if I had how would I have explained having them back if they had been nicked? It was just getting light before I drifted off, then all of a sudden I was woken by Sophie telling me I had to be at her house by four o'clock. Then she disappeared without giving me her address. I laid back down and tried to go back to sleep but it was useless. I was wide awake so I went through the bags again just in case I'd missed something and also to find something to wear to go to Sophie's. I needed a wash and to find a way to wash my hair. I didn't want to go to dinner smelling and looking like a tramp. In the bag I found a pair of shorts and a T shirt. I slipped them on and went for a swim in the sea, *the water was bloody freezing.* As long as I'd been there I never saw anyone in the sea. People must have thought I was crazy, swimming at the crack of dawn. I couldn't get any hot water and I didn't have any shampoo or toothpaste so I made the best out of a bad situation. I used one of the blankets to dry myself; I'd stolen a hairbrush a couple of weeks earlier, at least my hair wouldn't look dishevelled. It was time for me to be at Sophie's but I still had no address for her so I headed in a direction I thought she may live. As I was passing a B&B, a door opened and I heard a voice saying, "Aren't you coming in for dinner?" It was Sophie's Mum. I looked at her and wondered, were they just staying there or was it their home? If they wanted me to know then they would tell me. I didn't think it appropriate to ask because her mum might have thought I wanted to be her friend because they had money. I ended up going there twice a week for dinner. They asked me to go more often but I declined, I didn't want them to think I was taking advantage of their generosity and I couldn't put up with her mother more than that either. She was too obsessive, too overprotective and her best friend. It was like her mum was saying, "There can only be one best friend and that's me," without actually saying the words. I thought it extremely unnatural, however, that was fine by me I really didn't do the best friend thing anyway. There was no room in my life at this point in time for best friends. I preferred my own company most of the time and it was easier because I couldn't get hurt. It didn't take her mother long before she tried to control my life, telling me what to do, what to wear and what to say just as she did with Sophie. I was my own person and I wasn't having her telling me what to do. I did what I wanted and when I wanted. Because they knew where I was living, I decided to move on. I walked the streets of Portsmouth for days going down side streets and places I'd never been before looking for somewhere. I wasn't sure where, but then I found it!

As I searched the side streets and alleyways I came across a derelict house. It wasn't boarded up, but looked empty. I found a way in and had a good nosy around. The house had been used at some time; I don't know if squatters had been there but lying around was an old kettle and some metal cups and plates. There was an open fire as well. Just around a corner of the room I was in was also an old mattress. I stayed in the house what seemed like hours to see if anyone came but no one did. I made my mind up that this was the ideal place for me; everything I needed was in there. By the time I got back to the bridge, it was almost dark. I settled myself down for the night and started to write a letter to Sophie.

Dear Sophie,

I am sorry but there is no way that we can be friends. I find it hard to be myself around your mother and I don't like the way she has tried to take over my life. She is not my mother and you're not my sister. I have a family. Just because I find it hard to live with them doesn't mean they aren't still my family at the end of the day. It would be best if we never see each other again.

That's why I've moved away.

Yours

Street Girl

I then packed all my belongings in my bags ready for my move. When I woke up it was just getting light; this was the perfect time for me to go. No one was about and it was too early for Sophie to be up. I folded up my blankets tied them together with some string I'd found, and then I put the note where I knew Sophie would find it. I could have put it through her door but I wasn't sure if her mother would have been up. If she had would she have given it to Sophie? I didn't want to take that chance. I eventually got to the house;

I had another good look around to see if anyone was there or had been since the previous evening. Everything looked the same as I left it. I then set about trying to make it homely. I found some old pallets laying around so I gathered them up, put the mattress on top of them and arranged my blankets on it. *Hey presto a bed*. I took a walk to the shops which were nearby and, lucky for me I noticed an outside water tap. I turned it on quickly to see if it worked, *bingo I had water now*. I ran back to the house, grabbed hold of the kettle and went back to fill it. Back at the house it dawned on me I had nothing to make a drink with. I still had no money and I had to find a way to get some bits, it was going to be difficult. I could try begging again but that was a useless exercise last time people weren't really that generous. After a while I went into town, but as I was leaving the house I saw a milk float with no milkman. So I borrowed a pint of milk and a loaf of bread and quickly put them in the house before he came back and saw me. Then I went into town. I could have left him a note, one pint everyday please and a loaf every other day but he would have wanted paying for them so I didn't bother with that. While I was walking around, something on the pavement caught my eye. I bent down to have a look and it was a pound note. As I kept walking and looking down I was finding pennies so by the time I'd finished walking I'd got about three pounds in my pocket, *how lucky was I?* It wasn't quite enough for what I needed but an idea sprung to mind. I wasn't sure if it would work but nothing ventured, nothing gained. I went into the supermarket, spent the three pounds and bagged up the items. I asked the checkout lady for an extra bag which she gave me. I needed the bags because the shop's logo was on them. Further up the town there was another branch of that supermarket so I went into that one. Before I walked into the store, I split the bag of shopping I had into the two bags so now I had two half filled bags. I waited outside until someone went in and I'd walk in with them so it looked as if we were together. As I walked around looking for other things I may need and without anyone noticing I put the things into my bags. By the time I walked out of there without being caught, both my bags were full. I was expecting to be caught so I mingled with the crowds until I knew then I was in the clear. With the items I borrowed was a box of matches. It was a definite must I could now light the fire and make hot drinks. Now I would be able to keep warm at night. My first night in my own house had quite an eerie feeling but I soon fell asleep and slept like a baby, my first decent night's sleep in such a long time. It was light when I woke up but I had no idea what time it was. There were no passersby anymore to gauge the time by.

By now I'd been living on the streets for about six months. I knew deep down what I was doing was not right but there wasn't much more I could do. *Yeah,* I could have gone home but home to what? Bad memories, seeing all those demons all around and reliving everything that had happened to me. I really missed my family but I felt it had to be this way a little bit longer or until I got caught, whichever came first. Until that day arrived, I'd have to make the best out of a bad situation. Although I had hot water to wash with what I needed was the bits to go with the hot water. After I had made myself some toast on the open fire (*yummy*) and a drink, I went looking for more money. It's funny how lazy some people can be; they drop money and can't be bothered to pick it up! I couldn't complain; their loss my gain. As soon as I left the house, my head was bent down looking. Again I walked into town. There wasn't many people about, it was too early in the morning. I sat on a bench thinking to myself *this is the first morning in a long time I wasn't hungry and out borrowing from shops.* I scanned the area looking for money but it was still a bit too early. Soon the centre started to fill up with early morning bargain hunters. As they walked past they just stared at me. I watched them walking past me and thinking to myself *have I got two heads or something*. Then I heard a clang. I knew the sound it was a coin dropping, I looked around when all of a sudden I felt a tap on my shoulder. When I turned there was a policeman standing next to me. My only thought was I'd been caught. I looked at him waiting for him to take me in, but no he handed me the money just over five pounds. He must have thought I'd dropped it. I wasn't going to be foolish enough to say it wasn't mine, my needs were greater than the person who dropped it in the first place. I thanked the officer, put it in my pocket and moved to another bench still scanning the pavement. I started to get hungry and, having a few extra bob in my pocket, I treated myself to a burger. Time had gone so fast it was now four thirty and I only had a half hour before the shops shut. I quickly counted what I had left of the money I had found and there was almost seven pounds. I rushed to the supermarket and bought soap, a flannel, a toothbrush and some toothpaste, I still needed something to put hot water into so a trip to the charity shop was called for in the hopes I'd find something suitable to hold it. I found a large mixing bowl *that would do*, some towels and a couple of pans. Not really ideal for cooking on an open fire but they'd do for the time being and at least I'd have something hot inside me. All I needed now was cardboard which I obviously couldn't buy in there for the windows to stop the light coming in at sunrise. I managed to find some on my way home. When I got there the first thing I did was to put the kettle on to wash my hair and myself. While I was waiting for it to boil, I put the cardboard up against the windows. I lived like that for weeks it suited me. I could be by myself and I had no one to lie to. I got lonely at times but that was my fault I pushed everyone away.

One particular evening I went for a walk. The solitude was getting to me. Although I'd see people during the day the nights were different. I hadn't seen or spoken to anyone for over a month and just a simple hello would have been good. As I walked across the water front there were a few people who as I passed them, said, "good evening" and carried on walking. Before I knew it I'd walked to the harbour and I stood watching the calmness of the sea. I hadn't noticed the darkness falling; I must have been in a world of my own and, as I turned to walk away I got my foot caught in something, before I knew it I was in the drink! The bloody water was freezing. I was in dire straits as I could feel myself being pulled down and the weight of my clothes wasn't helping the situation, it took all of my strength to keep afloat. I decided at one point to give up then all my nightmares and torment would finally be over but something was telling me to fight. I then started to shout and cry for help! Two policemen were passing, heard my cries and came running down, I just managed to hear one of them call for an ambulance while the other one threw me a lifesaver. I could hardly feel my hands and only just managed to catch it. They were waiting for the ambulance so as they pulled me out, they wrapped something around me to keep me warm. The ambulance soon turned up and took me to St Mary's hospital so I could be checked out. I was kept in overnight for observation, I wasn't going to refuse a warm bed, hot drinks and a decent breakfast, who was I to complain? The next day, one of the officers came back to see me. They had found out who I was. They told me everybody was out looking for me and they thought it was time for me to go home to my family where I belonged. I wasn't having any of It. I was my own person and that's the way I wanted it to stay, but being relatively young there was no way he was going to let me back on to the streets. They sat with me for quite a long time, trying to persuade me it was in my best interest to go home. Only I knew what was best for me, or so I thought, and going home wasn't on my list. As the officer was leaving, he told me they were keeping me in for an extra night and that he'd be back tomorrow. True to his word, he came back but not on his own, he had a woman with him from social services. They were brought in because I was refusing to go home. I couldn't stay in hospital or at the police station so they found me a hostel down one of the side streets in Portsmouth. I don't know if hostel was the was the right word, hostile would describe it better. The residents looked like they'd come out of the nick all hard and tough. I didn't even know what it was called and I really wasn't that bothered because I had no intensions of staying there. The social worker failed to tell me that I'd only be in there one night and that I'd be moved somewhere else which would be more permanent. The woman who ran the hostel was a right one, she wanted to know the ins and outs of a ducks arse and if you didn't tell her what she wanted to know she would throw you a look. *If looks could kill I'd be dead now.* She really made you feel quite uneasy. I was only going to be there one night so I didn't care what she said or did. As soon as it was light, I would be looking for a way out of that hell hole. The next morning, as I was starting my reconnaissance, the bloody social worker turned up and told me she was moving me to another place in Winchester. I arrived at the new place, and yet again, I had no idea what it was called. Again I had no intension of staying there, although it was a nice enough place. But, being a free spirit, I needed to be free. It was going to be hard to escape from this place as there were only two doors the front and back. I would have to pass the reception area and there was always someone there to get to the main door. And to get to the back door I would have to pass the kitchen where the cook had a bird's eye view of the door If she wasn't in the kitchen then the bloody thing was locked, *how inconsiderate*! I checked out the windows, but they were all fixed so they would only open about three or four inches just enough to let some air in, *again how inconsiderate*. Obviously there was no way I could squeeze through those *I'm wasn't Twiggy*. I asked if I could go out but I was told I couldn't for the first two weeks and then after that only if I was supervised. If I needed money I'd have to earn it by doing jobs around the place. The other girls had their own little clicks and, being the newbie, I didn't fit in with them. Only one girl spoke to me, I didn't ask her name and she never told it to me. The only reason she spoke to me was to tell me how things were done and about the top dog, another nameless person. She was one of the click but I didn't know which one. I was advised that If the top dog wanted me to do something it would be best if I did it. *No one tells me what to do and if she thinks just because I was the new girl I'd bow down to her every demands she can think again* I thought to myself as she was about to find out. Top dog never spoke to anyone personally, she got her little lap dogs to do it for her. I'd been there almost a week when one of her lap dogs came to me with a message from the boss. That's what they called her. I didn't know who she was and I didn't give a dam either. The message was that I'd have to get into the office and get whatever money was in there and put it into the flowerpot in the window. I had until the morning to do it. I sent a message back "If you want something from the office then get it your bloody self," then I walked away. Within the hour I had a visit from at least five of her lap dogs. They had come to teach me a lesson but their attempt was thwarted by a member of staff walking in and wanting to know what was going on. One of them was a quick thinker and told the staff member that I was overheard telling another girl that the first chance

I got I was going to get as much money as I could out of the office and get away from here. I was quickly taken to the manageress' office where the staff member informed her of my supposed heist. I just stood there with my hands in my pockets. The manageress asked me, "What are you playing at?" I just looked at her and said, "Before I answer your questions, can you answer mine?" She agreed so I asked her. "Before I came here were there any incidents that happened that there was no answers to?" I could see she was thinking and by the look on her face the answer was yes, but she didn't admit to it. I then answered her question, "I am not playing any games and if you think I am then you better get the police in." She knew there was more to it than what I was saying but she just told me to leave the room. As I walked out of the room some of the other girls were outside. I just walked past them and laughed. Unbeknown to me and I guess the others as well the manageress' son was a policeman. She obviously asked him to call in and after she explained everything to him he came to see me. The only thing he wanted to know was who had put me up to it. What could I tell him? "The only thing I know was that she called herself the boss and that she sent messages through her entourage." He wanted to know if I could find out more for him and I told him that it was his job not mine. All I wanted was to be left alone. After he had gone, another girl came up to me and wanted to know what I had said. I told her there was nothing I could say and even if I did it had nothing to do with her. After that they all left me alone. I had one more week before I could start going out and all I had to do was to keep my head down. The time soon passed, that was the easy bit. The manageress' son came everyday to check on things and still was trying to find out who was responsible for all the other incidents. The manageress was now feeling guilty about blaming the other girls and moving them on when they could have been totally innocent. I would have loved to find out what the so called boss had on the other girls. None of them were talking and I still didn't know who the boss was, all I wanted to do was to get out of this god forsaken place.

The day finally arrived when I could go out but I still had to be accompanied by a member of staff. That didn't deter me from having a good look around, scanning the area and, as we passed a certain road, the stupid cow told me that the train station was down there, *how thoughtful of her and lucky for me*. All I now needed to do was to find a way of escaping. I was still doing my chores, earning money, and if I did everything that was asked of me they would let me out on my own sooner or later. It was sooner than I thought. After two weeks of keeping my head down I was allowed out by myself *whoopee*. I think some of it was the manageress feeling somewhat guilty. She told me that if I wanted to go into town without an escort then I could. I was playing the waiting game by now and told her I wasn't going to town this week but maybe next week. The following week I stayed out about an hour. I went to find the times of the trains back to Portsmouth. After another two weeks I was allowed out during the week. I proved I could be trusted not to run away and they didn't really know me. My plan was working. I managed to save quite a bit. One more week of doing what I was doing should be enough. I picked a Sunday to do my disappearing act, knowing most of them would be at church. I told them that I wasn't feeling too good and I was going to stay in bed. One of them offered to stay behind to look after me. I didn't find that too much of a problem because she would spend her time in the kitchen with the cook having a good old chin wag. The only problem I had was getting my timing right. I already had my things packed and hidden at the bottom of the stairs. About half an hour after everyone had gone, I went looking for the staff member. I and found her where I thought she'd be, in the kitchen. I knew she'd be in there for quite a while. This was my chance! I got my things and walked out of the front door and gate then I ran to the station. There was a train due but by the time I got there the train had gone, I'd missed it by minutes. The next one wasn't due for over an hour and by then the staff would be back from church and probably realise I was missing. I had to wait but I needed somewhere to hide. There wasn't anywhere on the platform or in the station for me to go so I had to take my chances. While I was sat there two police officers came onto the platform. I tried to avoid eye contact with them but it wasn't easy. They noticed me and realised I was trying to avoid them *body language is a terrible thing*, they came over to me and asked, "Where are you going?" Just as they were talking to me a voice came over their radio saying, "A girl has gone missing from the hostel," and then gave out a description. The officers started to walk away when one of them must have realised it was me. I was just about to leave when they grabbed hold of me, escorted me out of the station and back to the hostel. I was refusing to go back there; I told them if they took me back there I'd be off again the first chance I got. Well another night in the police cells, *it was becoming a bit of a habit doing the rounds of the countries police cells.* Because I wasn't under arrest they couldn't close or lock the cell doors. I was just being held for my own safety. Again, social services were informed and after the police had explained everything to them they agreed I was to be kept at the station overnight until they made other arrangements for me. The only place they could think of putting me was in a hostel in Nottingham. I heard through the grapevine that it was like a prison and nobody had ever escaped from there. Oh good, a challenge to prove them wrong! It was another waiting game to see what they were going to do with me in the morning. I had one of the best sleeps I'd had in a quite while, probably because I knew I was safe and nobody was going to attack me in the night. I felt like that in the police cells in Scotland. The morning soon came around. An officer woke me with a nice breakfast and then told me social services would soon be here and I would know my fate. Would they take me to Nottingham or would they put me somewhere else? I got stuck into my breakfast *oh boy did I enjoy it!* Then they gave me some hot water to have a wash. About eleven o'clock the social service lady turned up and said to me, "You're going to the hostel in Nottingham." Now I knew I definitely had a challenge to prove that I could escape from there. It would take about three to four hours to get there. The social worker wasn't very talkative which made the travelling very boring. I tried to see how many different makes of cars there were on the road but that bored the hell out of me. We stopped a couple of times and she still didn't talk so in the end I fell asleep for what I thought was a few minutes and when she woke me we had arrived at our destination. I looked around before I got out of the car. I knew then I wasn't going to like it there; the house looked cold and dreary it was an old building, the sort of house that someone with money back in the eighteen hundreds would have owned. As we entered the main door, a lady was standing there waiting to meet and greet us. She introduced herself as Mrs Hall and was telling us who some of the other members of staff were. The resident nurse was Miss Clarke and then there was the cook Mrs McCloud. There were so many members of staff I couldn't remember all their names. Mrs Hall seemed like a nice woman, but I learned never to take anything you see or hear at face value. Miss Clarke was a relatively old, never married and quite stern looking, *maybe that's why she never married no one would have her.* The cook, Mrs McCloud, was a jolly woman and always had a smile on her face. She was from Inverness and when I told her where I was from we got on like a house on fire. However, I didn't forget about my challenge to escape. I was beginning to feel like the character Steve McQueen played in the film The Great Escape. At the first opportunity I started to case the joint for possible exit routes. It wasn't going to be easy. I'd already been there two weeks and worked out that Mrs McCloud liked to pick her own fruit and veg from the local market and every Saturday she would pop down there, leaving the kitchen unattended for at least two hours. She never seemed to rush herself which I was pleased about. I put everything in place for the following Saturday and made sure I kept to my routine so no one would suspect. I was a dab hand at that after the last place I was in. I kept everything as normal as I could but as Saturday was approaching I started to get nervous. For the first time I was unsure about doing it. It could have been down to the fact that if I succeeded I would have been the first one to escape. The day arrived so I got my belongings together and hid them behind a chair in the dining room. I then went into the kitchen to say hello to Mrs McCloud and have our little chats as we did every day. She asked if I would like to go to the market with her. I declined the offer and sat there while she got ready to go then she asked me again I just shook my head. She was soon out of the door; it took me a couple of minutes to realise I was on my own and she'd forgotten to lock the back door, *lucky for me*. I looked around there was no one about it was all clear. I got my belongings as fast as I could and quickly got out of the back door. As I was about to go down the alley at the side of the house, I could hear someone coming the other way; I hid behind a shed and looked who it was, bloody hell it was Mrs McCloud she remembered she'd left the back door unlocked. *Too late I was out ha ha.*When she left again, I made my way up the alley, up to the

113

main gate and then I legged it as fast as I could. I didn't have a clue as to where I was going so I followed the sign for the town centre. Then I remembered the cook would be there, so I changed direction and found myself in the area of Sherwood Forest. It didn't take them long back at the house to notice I was missing and by nightfall the police had found me and yet again I refused to go back just as I did with all the other times. I didn't have a choice this time I had to go back there. The next day the social worker came to see me and I told her that there was no way I was staying here any longer than I had to and she agreed. Considering I'd escaped the inescapable they didn't want me back. *Why should they have me back? I'd proved them wrong,* that wasn't a good advert for them. I was found another place but I could only stay there until I was sixteen. It was nearer to my home so back on the road again. This social worker was a bit more talkative and asked me why I kept running away from all the hostels I told her that I was a free spirit and I needed to spread my wings. I felt like a bird trapped in a cage. I was going to Cowley in Oxford and because I only had two and a half months before my sixteenth birthday it was in my best interest to stay put until then. After that I could be as free as a bird but it depended on what it was like, and I hated all the others. She said "It's not a hostel it's a young person's shelter, a place where they get young people like you ready for the big wide world. They also teach you how to survive out there." What good would that do me and what could they teach me?" She obviously didn't know I'd been looking after myself for almost a year none of that information had been passed down to her. I explained almost everything to her, just the things I needed her to know and all she could say was, "You could help others." "No way unless I paid for it," I replied. She went quiet for the rest of the trip which suited me down to the ground. I didn't know what I was expecting to find when we got there but it looked the same as the others places I had to stay.

As it happened it was a nice place compared to the others. The rules were different; we could earn money from making soft toys to sell. We got a percentage of what we sold so it was really in my beat interest to get my hands going and to make as many as I could. We were also encouraged to make contact with our parents. I hadn't spoken to mine in over nine months but with the proper arrangements parents could visit. Mum and Henry did come to visit a few times but we were like strangers making polite conversation. Mum tried so hard but it was me, I wasn't ready for the mother daughter thing just yet. The bond we had was broken and had to be repaired, I would have had to tell her everything and I still wasn't ready to do that. Mum tried to get me to open up and the more she tried the more I dug my heels in.

Eventually I had to ask her to leave. It really upset her but I didn't want to go down that road yet and I wasn't sure I ever would. Only time would tell. I had already made my mind up to stick it out and it wasn't too long before my sixteenth birthday when at that time the people at the shelter would help me find a place to live and pay the first two months rent and also help with anything else I needed to set up home. I had to do the same with the money I earned from making the toys, I didn't earn a great deal because I hadn't been there long. I didn't know Henry was sending them money each week to help me buy things for when I eventually got a place of my own.

My sixteenth was here. I received a few cards from the other girls and the staff at the shelter but not from Mum. However, the postman hadn't been yet. I waited in anticipation but there wasn't anything for me when he eventually delivered. I couldn't blame mum I treated her appallingly. I just sat there in a world of my own until a member of staff came and told me I had visitors. As I walked into the reception area I started to get very nervous who could it be? Nothing had been arranged but there they were Mum and Henry all dressed up to the nines. Henry had his suit on looking really smart and Mum looked pretty, just like she did when she got dressed up for church in Scotland. I asked them, "What are you doing here?" and for the first time Henry spoke first. He said "We're here for your birthday and we are taking you out for lunch, it's all been arranged." I said to them "I can't go because I've nothing to wear, you've made a great effort for me and I don't want to show you up by looking like a tramp." Mum passed me a present with cards, and as I opened the cards I began to cry. The words were so beautiful. Then I opened my present. It was an outfit and a pair of shoes. Mum had got the staff to get my sizes. Seeing those beautiful presents made me ashamed of myself for everything I had done. I couldn't turn back time; all I could do was to try to move forwards and somehow try to repair the damage I had caused. Making a start I got myself ready for to take me out for lunch.

We seemed to have been driving a long time when we eventually stopped at a pub restaurant in the middle of nowhere called the Green Man. As we sat and ate Mum tried to start up a conversation. She had so many questions and I had so much to tell her. Lew, Andy, the man in Birmingham and baby Charlotte but I still had the same problem. How could I tell her and would she believe me? Henry started to talk about himself which was good. He took the conversation away from me so I didn't have to start answering awkward questions. He also talked about the rest of the family. And he told me that Alan had been around every day since I left to see if there was any news and he was also desperate to see me. I wasn't sure about that one yet. We all had a lovely afternoon and as they dropped me back at the shelter, Henry asked me to come back home. I said "No, it's not your place to ask me it is Mum's." *Considering she never asked me I assumed she didn't want me back because I was trouble.* I'd convinced myself that there was no way of repairing the damage now, Mum went to give me a cuddle but I stepped back. How could I give someone a cuddle who didn't want me? I could see tears in her eyes but was it tears for the way she felt or for not giving me a cuddle?

I didn't ask I just walked away. As I reached the front door, I turned to see Henry trying to comfort her. Some of the girls saw what had happened and thought I was a cold, heartless bitch, but what did they know? For four years I had to keep my feelings and emotions locked up inside of me. I know found it hard to let them out, they didn't know my story so. They had no right to judge me and I told them so. I needed to know when I was getting my own place. I asked various members of the staff but no one seemed to know, the only person who did know had finished for the day so I had to wait until she came back on duty. The next day I went looking for her and asked, "When am I getting my own place." "I don't think you're ready for it just yet but they have found you a shelter for over sixteen's. You'll be going there tomorrow, so go and start packing." She wanted to know if she should inform my parents, I said, "No." I didn't have any intensions of staying there and as for me not being ready, I was more than ready, more ready than most of the other girls in there. The next day my things were put into a car and as I was about to walk out of the door when one of the staff handed me an envelope. It was a bit thick; I just slung it into a carrier bag and would open it when I was on my own. I arrived at the other place. It was two houses joined together and could only house six at a time. Just like the other places I wasn't going to stay here either. This wasn't what I agreed on. I was shown my room and told to unpack as lunch was almost ready. We didn't have a cook so we had to cook for ourselves. It was good for those who needed it but that wasn't me. I decided not to unpack; it would save time when I did my vanishing act again. I sat on the bed looking around, just wasting time when I suddenly remembered the envelope. I opened it to find a letter from all the staff wishing me good luck and some money with another letter explaining where it had come from. Some of the money was from what I had earned and the rest of it came from Mum and Henry. I counted it and there was just over a hundred pounds, *oh my God I was a millionaire*. I had never seen so much money before let alone have so much of it. I hid it and then went down to lunch. I was introduced to the rest of the girls. It was pointless really. It all went in one ear and out of the other. I wasn't interested in them and we certainly wouldn't be friends. Everyone was sat around eating. They were all chatting away and even tried to engage me in conversation but I wasn't having any of it. In the end I just went back to my room. A member of staff came up to see if I was alright. I told her I was fine and that's how it was for three days by the fourth day I'd had enough, I had to get out of there so I waited until everyone was asleep and just walked out of the back door. It was that easy. I found my way to the train station, this time it was different there would be no police trying to find me. I was legally old enough to leave home. I managed to get the last train back to where it all started and booked into a B&B for the night. It was too late to do anything else and in the morning I would decide what my next step would be.

When I woke up I had my breakfast then I went looking for a bedsit. I found one on the other side of the train station and hoped I had enough money for at least two weeks rent which I did. After I moved in I went to the Citizens Advice

Bureau to find out if there was anyone or anywhere that could help me pay my rent. They told me there was a place at the council that helped people like me and I could also get help from Social Security. I had my own place now and I was all legal. Mum and Henry found out what I had done and they came round to see me and try to get me to come back home. I still refused so they did everything they could to help me. Henry tried to give me money but I always refused it. Mum bought me the things I needed, cutlery, dishes, pots and bedding. I had some of those things already but it didn't matter you can't have enough of those things anyway. I even went for my dinner twice a week to Mum's hoping to repair some of the damage I had caused all those months ago. I even met up with Alan again but this time he wanted us to be a couple. I agreed on one condition that we would take things slowly and we would only see each other every other day to start with. We would see each other in the bedsit while other people were going in and out of the building he agreed to that. He soon made friends with the other tenants. There was one person I got on really well with, a bloke called Tom. He came from Scotland, that's probably why I got on so well with him. The three of us would all go out at weekends, both men got on extremely well which was great because Alan knew when he wasn't around, Tom would look out for me.

CHAPTER 7
MUM AND HENRY'S WEDDING

Things were starting to look up for me now. I had a place of my own, friends and I was in a relationship which I never thought I would have. I can't say I loved him but what is love?

Something didn't feel right; I put it down to my past experiences and I thought that after some time had passed, what I was feeling would change. But, time would tell. I carried on with my life the best way I could, I celebrated my seventeenth birthday with Alan and our friends. Henry was still trying to get me to move back home and I was still declining his offer. Things were improving and Alan and me were talking about moving in together, but there was one major problem; his mum. Every time he talked to her about it she would come down ill with something or another she'd go as far as to say she'd been to the doctors and he recommended bed rest and this went on for months. We spent Christmas apart because of her.

She didn't like me and thought I was after him for his money, *that made me laugh he didn't have any!* He worked but all his money went on supporting her. I didn't think she was evil, just lonely and if Alan moved out, she'd be on her own.

Christmas had come and gone. 1978 was here and I was hoping it would be a new beginning. Mum and I were getting along much better now and on one of my weekly visits we were sat talking. She kept looking at me funny; I said "Is there a problem?" She said "No," then a short time later she wanted to know if I was feeling okay. I thought it was a strange question so I told her I was fine. Then Mum asked me "When's the baby due?" "What baby" I replied" The one you're carrying" Mum said "I'm not expecting" Yes you are" she replied, "don't be bloody silly Mum I'm on the pill so I can't be," However, it got me thinking that just maybe that's why from time to time I felt a little unwell. So, to be on the safe side, I got checked out and by George she was right, *don't you just hate it when mothers are always right?* I was only a few weeks so I decided not to say anything to anyone; mind you, I didn't need to say anything to Mum she already knew! Of course I told Alan he was going to be a daddy and he was over the moon at the idea of having a child. I told him not to say anything, but he opened his gob to his mother and that's when things changed. Over a few days his mum managed to convince him that the baby wasn't his and I'd been seen out with a coloured man so the baby must be his. Later that day, Alan came to see me and told me that we needed to talk. We went for a walk and it was then he told me he didn't want anything to do with me or the baby because it wasn't his baby it was the coloured mans whom I'd been seeing. I couldn't believe what I was hearing. It didn't matter what I said, his mother had done a good job in brain washing him, *what an evil woman*. I said to him, "If that's the way it's going to be then maybe it's for the best." then I walked away. I went back to my bedsit and cried my eyes out, *what was I going to do with a baby and not having it's father by our sides?* Tom soon stepped in and said, "I'll stand by you." *Bless him*. I didn't want that. He was only a friend and that's all but how was I tell to him that without hurting his feelings? I came to the conclusion the best way was to come straight out with it. He seemed to take it okay and said, "As a friend I'll still be there for you." *God love him*. When everything had calmed down, I tried talking to Alan again. He just walked away. I still hadn't told anyone. I needed time to decide what I was going to do. It was still early days and I had a few options to choose from but I had to choose the best one for me. I'd applied to go into the R.A.F and passed all the tests and the medical, I was just waiting on them sending me the date to go in. I was in a right dilemma; career or child? An abortion wasn't an option I didn't believe in that, so was it adoption or bring it up myself? The answer was slapping me in the face; I'd already lost one child and I couldn't bear to lose another one. It was an easy answer. I was keeping it. Still nobody knew about Charlotte and no one would if I could help it.

I was three months gone by now and starting to show. Tom came round to see if I wanted to go for a drink I said, " Yes just as friends." We went to our local and I had soft drinks but Tom was knocking them back as though there was no tomorrow. I asked him to slow down but all he could say was, "it's none of your business." Then he hit me! I wasn't going to stand for that so I did no more than to pick his pint up, poured it over his head and walk out. He followed me outside, got hold of me and started to verbally abuse me but when I started to argue back he hit me and then he started beating me. He even tried to kick me in the stomach. The police arrived and he told the officers to get lost and not to interfere in a domestic, *how could he say that when we weren't a couple?* The police officers were just about to walk away when I called him back. I had to ask "How could it be classed as a domestic if we are only friends?" They looked bemused and one of them told me that if that was the case then it's assault. He took me to his car and I explained everything that happened; that we were not a couple and I was just over three months pregnant. Tom was then arrested for assault and endangering a life. I was then taken to hospital to be checked out. I had some bruising but luckily enough everything was fine. The next day the police came to see me for my statement and told me he had been charged but he was denying it all. He had been released on police bail and there was a possibility I may have to attend court.

After the officer had left I sat and looked around, *was this the sort of place I wanted to bring a child back to?* I had too much time to think. After Tom had been charged nobody wanted to know me, it was if they blamed me. He was a nut case and the father of my child didn't want to know. I was all on my own; again I had to get out of those four walls so I went to see Mum and Henry. As I walked through her front door, Mum was horrified to see me with a black eye *I looked as though I'd gone ten rounds with Henry Cooper.* She obviously wanted to know how I got it so I explained everything to her, she asked, "Are you okay?" I said I was but deep down I wasn't but I was too scared to admit it. I think Henry knew by the way he looked at me. He'd had enough and told me straight that I was going down the wrong road. I had no idea what he was going on about and he mentioned about moving back home, this time he made me feel as though I didn't have a choice, on reflection he was right. I needed all the support I could get so I agreed to stay the night. The next day he took me to collect my belongings. As it happened it worked out to be the best move I'd made in years. Mum had already got a grandchild from Tess, but she seemed to be more excited about mine. I asked her why. She couldn't give me answer, all she kept saying was, "This one is different." She couldn't explain what she meant apart from she had a feeling. Mum made sure I ate properly and kept all my doctor's appointments. I felt I was carrying the child for her and I felt this happened too quickly, I also felt she was smothering me, I just lost my temper and told her she needed to take a step back and to let me breathe or else I'd have no choice but to move back out. Neither of them wanted me to do that.

One day Henry called a family meeting; it was the only way he could get all of us together in one room. He had something he wanted to ask us all, we all sat down. Henry left the room for a minute and when he came back he stood near to Mum and then started to tell us how much he loved this woman, that he'd do anything for her and would never do anything to hurt her. Then he turned to us all and asked us individually for our permission to marry her. When it came to me I just said, "You don't need our permission Mum is an adult in her own right and if she is happy, and that's what she wants what right do we have to stand in her way?" Henry got down on one knee and asked her in front of us all for her hand in marriage, *how romantic,* Mum looked at us all and we all nodded then she said, "Yes." The look on his face said it all; she had just made him the happiest man alive. His smile made him look like the cat who got all the cream. He was like that all day *bless him.* They could only have a registry office wedding because of Mum being a divorcee but they weren't bothered as long as they were together. The date was set for October. While they were preparing for that, I was getting ready for my little one to come into the world. I kept being told that everything was going well but I still had a great fear I was going to lose this one as well. Henry could tell I was worried about something but I couldn't tell them about Charlotte. As time went on I was getting so much bigger and people thought I was carrying twins. When I sat down to eat, I used my belly as a tray and put my plate on it. My due date came but there was no sign of the little one appearing. Henry had a Hillman Imp I think it was. You could feel every bump and pot hole you went over so Henry had a brain wave. To try to start my labour off, he'd take me out in his car and drive over every bump and pothole he could find but that didn't do the trick. I tried a few of the old wives tales to try to bring on my labour like having a hot bath after drinking cod liver oil but nothing I tried seemed to work so it was just the waiting game until the little one decided it was time to see the outside world. I had everything packed and ready to go.

Back to the wedding plans and getting the final bits organised. Midsummer was here and I woke up one morning with a bad stomach. I was in the early stages of labour then I wet the bed; my waters had broke. I told Mum that it was time for us to get to the hospital and Henry was like a big woman flapping around, not sure what to do. In the end Mum snapped and told him to get the car. At the hospital Mum was as much use as a chocolate tea pot. She spent more time talking to the doctor that she did me. There I was in pain but *it was like watching a comedy act at the bottom of my bed*. Mum and the doctor were putting on bets to see what sex, weight and time it would arrive. The doctor was convinced it was going to be a boy arriving at ten past two and Mum said, " It's going to be a girl weighing just over eight pounds and arriving at ten past three." Just past three p.m. my beautiful daughter arrived weighing just over eight pounds. I had to have a few stitches, twenty four to be precise. I had to ask if they thought I was a dart board, I felt every prick! Back on the ward I couldn't take my eyes off her. She was so delicate, just like a piece of china. Her skin was so soft, she had blonde hair and blue eyes she was perfect. I couldn't decide on a name. If it had been a boy then I would have named him Charles after Henry's dad but it was a girl and I couldn't think of a name for her just yet. I was kept in hospital for a week which was normal back then. After I got home I got us both into a routine. I was determined to do it all by myself. I still didn't have a name for her as yet but I had six weeks to register her birth. However, I needed her birth certificate so I could sort out the child benefit and income support. I named her Chantelle.

The day I took Chantelle to be registered I spotted Alan going to his auntie's, I was going to call him over but changed my mind. I thought I'd wait until he got there. I wrapped her up in a blanket and told Mum what I was doing. She thought I would be wasting my time, *I probably was but he had to know the truth*. At the end of the day it was up to him. I walked to his auntie's and asked if I could see him. She was just about to say he wasn't there when he came to the door and said, "What do you want?" I told him I'd brought his daughter to see him but the way I had her wrapped up he couldn't see her face and he said, "The little black bitch isn't mine." I looked at him in disgust, pulled the blanket off her face and said to him " Have a good look and remember what she looks like because the next time you see her is if and when she wants to meet you." He threatened me with court; I told him to, "Go ahead even if the courts gave you your rights, I would go against them, no one calls my baby a little black bitch and I will tell the court that. Go ahead and do your worse." His aunty wanted to see her but I refused. She was no better than he was so I just walked away. They did everything they could to make me change my mind but nothing was going to do that and I went as far as to tell them they weren't good enough to be called a family. I might have been a bit harsh but to me he got what he deserved, and his mother was still saying she was a black man's baby. The way I looked at it they were the ones losing out. I had a beautiful daughter to be proud of. However, they had a daughter, granddaughter and niece they would know nothing about.

They wouldn't be there for her milestones, her first tooth, sitting up, crawling, walking, her first word and most importantly her first day at school all because his mother brain washed him. There were only a few weeks to go before the wedding and we were all excited. Mum and Henry agreed it would just be the immediate family and a sit down meal. Afterwards, all their friends were invited to the evening do and everything was going to plan. Me and the others were deciding on what we were wearing *choices, choices, choice, what do I wear?* The next day I received a letter from Alan stating that if I didn't let him see Chantelle, he would have no choice than to put in for full custody. I had to laugh. I found it highly amusing that one minute he denied the baby was his and the next minute he's going for full custody. I told Henry about the letter and he said, "let him try it would be over our dead bodies." Then he advised me to get a solicitor. I didn't get one; however I did get the legalities of it all from one. He told me that as the father Alan had rights but if I could prove he was unfit to have the child he wouldn't stand a chance of getting custody. When I got back home, I told Mum and Henry what the solicitor had said to me and all I needed was proof, so I started to ask around to see if he'd said anything to anyone. He was overheard saying, "She's a cunt and a slag and I wouldn't be surprised if she'd been charging men for sex. All the men were black, so if she's going to pass the little black bastard off as mine she can think again. I'm not going to raise some little nigger. *What a charmer!* At least four people heard him saying this so I asked these people if they would write it all down in their own words for me. They all agreed. After I got the statements from them I went to see Alan and showed him one of them. I told him that if he pursued this matter and continue with the threats I'd have no choice than to produce it in court. He snatched it out of my hand and ripped it up and said "Now you don't have proof." *the stupid git didn't know I had three more from different people*. I told him that it was a photo copy and I had at least another three saying the same. He walked away and I heard nothing from him after that *thank God* .I saw his mother once while I was out with Chantelle; she came across to try to see her I said to her, "Sling your hook. The child has nothing to do with you and that was the choice you made by telling all those untruths about me."

The day of the wedding was now here. It was a really cold October day with snow on the ground and I was worried about Chantelle as she was running a bit of a temperature. I rang the doctor to see if I could get a home visit because she was only six weeks old. I explained the symptoms to him and he told me to bring her to the surgery. I asked if he could visit her and again he told me to bring her to the surgery for eleven o'clock. When I told Mum and Henry, they were both fuming. He got straight on the phone and gave the doctor a right ear bashing. While he was doing that, I got ready, wrapped little lady to keep her warm and then Henry drove me to the surgery. Half an hour later we got called in to see the doctor. He examined her and told me it was just a cold and there was nothing he could give me for it. As we were about to leave his room he said, " A typical first time mother, over reacting at the slightest thing and all you did was waste my time when I could have been seeing someone who was really ill."I thought Henry was going to hit him but he just said, "You haven't heard the last of this. "I wondered what he meant so on the way home I asked him he said to me "After the wedding first thing in the morning I'll be ringing to make a formal complaint. I can't do it until then because the office I need is closed, don't worry I'll be dealing with it."

When we got home we explained everything to Mum and then arranged a babysitter. I couldn't and wouldn't take her as it was too cold. I told the sitter as soon as we'd eaten I'd be straight back, she said, "Don't worry and enjoy yourself. "I couldn't help it I had to keep phoning to see how Chantelle was. The sitter kept telling me she was fine.

The reception was held in the function room at the local pub so, after the meal, we all went into the bar. After a while, I told Mum I was going home and she told me to stay. Mum and Henry were going back because they wanted a bit of time together so they would look after her. Before she left Mum pointed to a man sat at the end of the bar and told me he'd been watching me all night. I told her she was seeing things and not to be stupid. She just laughed and walked out of the door with her husband at her side .I needed to sit down and have a few minutes for myself. Then all of a sudden, I started to think back to my life on the streets and how I never gave my family a second thought. I guess I blamed Mum for what Lew had done to me. If she hadn't gone to prison it probably wouldn't have happened. It was so easy for me to switch off and not think about her when she met me at the train station. It was easy for me not to show any emotions which came in handy in years to come. The man from the end of the bar came over to talk to me. His name was Dan and Mum was right he had been watching me all night and trying to get my attention. He sat with me and we talked about anything and everything for the rest of the night. At the end of the night he, walked me home and told me he wanted to see me again. I wasn't sure if I wanted to or if I was ready for another relationship after Alan. Dan was like a bad smell. He kept coming back and wasn't taking no for an answer. Every day after work he'd come to see me and Chantelle and, as we talked he would play with her and sometimes, if she was asleep, he would wake her. You could see this beautiful bond forming between them and from the love he had for her, anyone would have thought he was the father. Even I had to remind myself he wasn't! By the beginning of December, I gave in to him and we became a couple. Alan found out and wasn't happy that Dan was bringing up his daughter *Alan had his chance and blew it*. He wrote me a letter stating his disapproval but I just ripped it up and disposed of it. As far as I was concerned, it had nothing to do with him now.

Christmas week was here and Dan turned up laden with gifts. Mum had already put the tree up and as usual it looked beautiful with all the baubles, tinsel and lights just like the ones on Christmas cards. Dan passed me the gifts to put under it and I noticed that most of them were for Chantelle. She was one little lady that wanted for nothing at three and a half months old and she wouldn't get bored with the amount of toys everyone bought her! By the New Year Mum said that Dan might as well move in with us all if that's what he wanted to do. I said "no it is still early days and I'd rather leave things the way they are for the time being." I'd let him stay twice a week, I wasn't ready for a full on relationship yet.

We were half way through January when Tess made one of her visits. When she visited, she was usually after something but this time it was different. It wasn't Mum or Henry she was after it was me which I found that rather odd. We sat talking normal chit chat small talk, "How you are you?" So on and so on. Then the real reason came out. She wanted to know what I was playing at. Well she had me totally confused. I had no idea what the hell she was going on about but Tess was like that she'd say something and expect you to know what she was going on about. I said to her, "I'm not a bloody mind reader and what the hell are you going on about?" She wanted to know why I was seeing Dan. Now I was totally and utterly confused. I asked her "why do you want to know? What right do you have to question who I go out with?" It just happened that Dan was the brother of Tess' husband and he'd recently moved into the area. It was the first time in ten years that the brothers had met and were just getting to know each other all over again. So according to Tess, I had no right coming between them. Mum and me just looked at each other. We had no idea and Dan never mentioned it. I told Tess but she called me a liar she then told me I had to stop seeing him and let the brothers have a chance to catch up. I couldn't believe what she was saying or demanding *Hitler had nothing on her*. I told her in no uncertain terms. "If me seeing Dan was coming between them then it was up to Dan and his brother. It had nothing to do with me." I only saw Dan four nights a week and two of those nights he stayed over (which we both agreed on) so he had the other three nights to catch up with his brother. But again, Tess told me to stop seeing him, I said, "I don't think so he's moving in soon." She got up and left. She was absolutely fuming and her blood must have reached boiling point. That night, when Dan came round, I asked him why he hadn't said who he was. He explained he wanted me to get to know him for who he was and not the brother of Glen. With that in mind, I told him if he was ready he could move in but only if he really wanted to. He just wanted things to stay as they were for the time being because he didn't want to rush me. He said for him to move in just after Tess had visited would be the wrong reason. *What a sensible man*, we came to conclusion that it would be better to wait a bit longer.

When Chantelle was born, I put my name on the housing list at the council but, because I was living with Mum it took longer than it would normally do. Luckily she had plenty of room. Maybe Dan would be different if I had my own place, so every week I phoned them to see how far up the housing list I was. I didn't seem to move and all they said was, "When it's your time, we'll find you the appropriate housing."

By the time April came, Tess was used to the idea of my relationship with Dan and whatever she said didn't make a blind bit of a difference. I also found out I was expecting again. I told Mum and Henry and made them promise not to say anything until I had the chance to tell Dan. It wasn't his night to visit so I had to decide whether to wait one more day or phone him to come round. He might have had plans so I decided to wait. I sat with Mum and Henry, discussing it and Mum asked me, "What will you do if Dan ends up the same as Alan, deny the baby is his and up sticks and leave? How would you cope with two kids?" It made me think of the possibility that it could happen but I couldn't think like that. I still hadn't told him but if that was the case I'd have to cope just like she did with six of us. Mum then came out with, "If that did happen, me and Henry could adopt Chantelle." I couldn't believe what she had just said and by the look on Henry's face neither could he. It was obvious they never discussed it. If they had, then he hid it well. I told them both straight that the only way they would get Chantelle was if I had an accident, I couldn't look after her or if I was dead. With that I went off to bed. I tossed and turned all night. It was playing on my mind and I even went down stairs clock watching for a couple of hours. Tonight was the night for me to see Dan and I could hardly wait for him to turn up. I needed to know how he felt about the situation because we never discussed starting a family together. All day I tried to avoid Mum but it was difficult so I stayed in my room for most of it only leaving it to either get Chantelle her bottle or go to the toilet. That was the only way I could avoid saying something to Mum that I'd probably regret. Dan was having dinner with us so he came round a bit earlier. He could tell something wasn't right you could cut the atmosphere with a knife. He could tell Mum wanted to say something during the meal. I was just about to clear the table when Henry said that he'd do it. It was his way of telling me to talk to Dan. I told Dan that we needed to talk but not here which didn't please Mum she obviously thought I was going to talk in front of her. I was nearly nineteen so it really had nothing to do with her. I was an adult in my own right. I think she wanted control over the conversation but that wasn't going to happen. Henry watched Chantelle while we talked alone. We were going to go for a drive but decided to sit in the car. I felt trapped so we went for a walk instead. I asked him how he felt about starting a family. He wouldn't mind starting one but not yet because it was still early in our relationship and he'd rather make sure that we were settled in our own home. He wanted to know why I brought the subject up now. I told him I was expecting and was six weeks gone. I also told him that if wasn't ready and wanted out that was fine and I would manage but before I could say anything else, he put his hand over my mouth to shut me up and then picked me up and held me for as long as he could. The look of delight on his face told me what I needed to know. We talked a little longer about the future and then went back to Mum's. When we got back there, and before she could say anything, Dan picked up Chantelle, gave her the biggest hug ever and told her she was going to have a brother or sister to play with. At least it showed Mum he wasn't going anywhere and any control she thought she had was gone. We decided to wait until I was three months gone before we told anyone else. In the meantime, I needed to push the council for my own place. I rang them and informed them of change of circumstances and they told me I'd be moved up the list and I wouldn't have too long to wait. Now, I could start getting things for my new house and baby. Weeks passed and turned into months but there was still no sign of a house. I kept phoning them and I even went into their offices trying to get them to understand how urgent it was. I needed a house quickly but it was obvious I wasn't saying the right things.

The next day, Tess rang them on my behalf. She told them that I only had a month to go, that the place needed to be decorated before the baby arrived and that Mum had given me two weeks to move out then I'd be on the streets. It did the trick. A couple of days later I received a letter telling me they'd found me a property. However, there was still all the decorating to do. I couldn't wait for the council to come and do it so I decided to do it all myself. The council would supply the materials needed and give me four weeks rent free. Most of the family rallied round and Mum and Henry were there every day. It didn't take long before it was ready for me and Chantelle to move into.

It was strange at first, just me and Chantelle on our own, especially staying at Mum's with people in and out most of the time. But it wouldn't be long before the patter of tiny feet would keep me busy along with little lady during the day. Dan was still unsure about moving in so things stayed the same with him. I did all the house work in the evenings while Chantelle was in bed, leaving the days for me to play with her or take her out. It was coming up to her first birthday so I thought I'd do a little tea party for her. I didn't know any of the neighbours or if any of them had any little ones so it was just Tess' two boys, Samuel and Steven, Mum and Henry, Tess didn't think much of it, I said to her, "If you don't like it then you know where the door is." She got her two together and left. Mum took her side and told me that I shouldn't have said that to her. She was in my house and she should have kept her opinions to herself. I'd done the best with what I had. I was just about to say a lot more when Mum decided it was time to go. On the way out, Henry said, "I agree with you and I'll try to sort something out." He could sense there was trouble on the horizon; I just said,

"Don't bother." I appreciated them helping with the decorating but Mum needed to remember that it wasn't her house, it was mine, and the rules changed once I moved out of hers if people couldn't respect me or my house then they weren't welcome.

Dan came up that night and told me he had something to ask so I went to make us some drinks. As I was doing that, he started pacing *bloody hell he was wearing the carpet out* he seemed a bit edgy. I said to him "If you've got something to say then you better do it now." I was expecting him to say it was over, how wrong was I? He got down on one knee and proposed, *how sweet!* I had to say no, I wasn't ready for it and I didn't think Dan was either. He couldn't commit to moving in and we'd only been seeing each other less than a year. Just because I was carrying his baby was no reason for us to wed. I explained this to him and he seemed to understand so we agreed to wait another year, for him to move in and for us to start living as a family. That way we'd know if marriage was the right thing for us. A few days later he moved in. We were a proper family now. I kept house and Dan worked. A week later I went into labour. Everything was ready, bag packed, Mum and Henry would have Chantelle and Dan would be with me. He phoned the hospital and told them the contractions were at least fifteen minutes apart. I had to go in when they were five minutes apart, *loads of time to get Mum and Henry here or* so I thought. Within half an hour, my contractions had gone to six minutes apart and Mum and Henry had to get a spurt on. By the time they arrived I was almost out of the door. They were now four minutes apart so it wouldn't be long before I had the urge to push. Within two hours of getting on to the labour ward, I gave birth to a Son. Dan was over the moon he now had a son and a daughter. I was concerned about Chantelle being at Mums after what she said about adopting her. Would she go behind my back? I had to stay in hospital for three days. The next day Dan brought Chantelle in to see me and said, "I've taken her back home where she belongs and I'm looking after her until you come home." I was worrying over nothing. I asked him about his job and he told me his boss had given him two weeks off, *that was nice of him.* The three days I was in, Dan came every day with Chantelle. She was beginning to bond with her little brother. She loved him and, with the cuddles I gave her she didn't feel left out. We named the little fella Raymond. Dan was still off work so getting into a routine wasn't too bad, *would I be able to cope on my own?*

When he went back to work, everything fell into place I had my routine down to a fine art. I played with little lady in between feeding and changing Raymond *what was I worried about?* Life was going well for the both of us. A beautiful home, two beautiful children what else did we need? Something was missing and I didn't know what and Dan seemed to be changing. He was always moody but I put it down to work. One day he came home from work in one hell of a mood. I asked, "Is there a problem?" he said no. After that day all we did was argue over petty little things, the kids toys on the floor, his dinner not quite being ready or the kids crying, things that never bothered him before. I told him if there was a problem at work leave it there, because it wasn't any good for the kids to hear us arguing day after day and being at each other's throats. He agreed and said, "I'll try." The following day when he walked in, the first thing he said was "Why is the house a mess? I take it you've been sat on your big fat arse all day?" I couldn't believe what I'd heard, "With two children no chance of doing that." I said, "What the hell is your problem?" Then, he just walked out. While he was out, I tidied up and started dinner thinking he'd cool off and be back by the time dinner was ready but there was no sign of him so I bathed the kids and got them ready for bed. I spent most of the night looking out of the window for him. I was just about to go to bed when he came in. I asked him if he wanted something to eat and where'd he'd been but he just ignored me and went to bed. *How ignorant.* The following day was the same I was beginning to wonder if was it worth him being here. We were meant to be a family! Then, I started to question myself. Did I have any feelings towards him? I wasn't sure then I put it down to being tired and having a baby and a toddler so maybe a good night's sleep would clear my mind. In the morning, I looked at him with the children. There was something there, was it love and was it enough to make the relationship work? I didn't know but I had to give it a chance. After two weeks, it was back to arguing again. I asked him, "Do you want to be with us or are you just here because of the children?" He avoided the question and went out. When he came back, there was something different about him but I couldn't put my finger on It. No questions this time, I just went to bed. Something woke me in the early hours. It wasn't the baby and there was no sign of Dan in bed. I ventured downstairs and he wasn't there either. Then I realised it was the front door closing that I heard. I put the bolts on the door because it wasn't secure enough without them and I didn't care if he could get back in or not. I hardly slept a wink the rest of the night waiting for him to knock but he didn't. When he eventually turned up, he wanted to know why I locked him out. As I tried to explain about securing the door he hit me across the face. I questioned his action and he started to hit me more in front of the children. I could hear Chantelle and Raymond crying but I couldn't get to either of them. Eventually he stopped and walked out of the door. I grabbed my babies and cuddled them while I was wondering what on earth had just happened, why had he changed and most importantly what was I going to do about it? All I knew was he would never lay another finger on me again and there was no way on earth I was going to subject my kids to the fear and abuse I had as a child from my father. My mother may not have been strong enough at that time but I wasn't her. I took the kids to Mum's and asked her if she could have them overnight. I explained why but an explanation wasn't necessary the marks on me said it all. Mum and Henry agreed to have the little ones. Henry wanted to know if I wanted him to come back with me but I declined. I told him that it was my problem to deal with. When I got back home, I put all Dan's clothes into bin bags and put them on the front door step. Then I secured all the doors and windows and I waited. It seemed like hours then I heard his key in the door. When he couldn't open it, he went around trying the back door. He came back to the front again and knocked. I told him it was over and his clothes were in the bag on the step but he kept knocking. Then the letter box opened, "I'm sorry, I love you, it won't happen again." he said. I replied "If you really love me then you wouldn't have done it and, as for not doing it again, you will never get the chance. I'm not letting you in." Then came the shouting and the name calling and him trying to kick the front door in. Then there was a different man's voice, he said "it's the police." At first I didn't believe him I thought Dan had got one of his mates to pretend so I'd open the door. I told him where to go then he told me to look out of my window. It was the police two of them, they had Dan in handcuffs near their car. It was only then I opened the door. There was also a policewoman with them whom I didn't see at first. One of the officers and the police woman came in to see if the kids were in the house. Apparently, two little old ladies who lived next door heard the commotion and called the police thinking that the kids were in the house *having nosy neighbours comes in handy*. I explained to the officers what had happened and they wanted to know where my kids were. I told them they were at my Mum's. They wanted to know if I wanted to press charges but I refused, I just wanted him out of my life. He was still taken into custody and kept overnight. After they had left, I went to stay at Mum's for the night. Before he was released, he was cautioned, told to stay away from me and if they had to come out to him again he would be arrested and charged and I wouldn't have a say in the matter. He proved that he had no interest in his son. He never tried to see him; he didn't even try to find out how he was doing. *Well here I am again on my own this time with two children.*

It didn't take long for things to get back to normal. The kids were happy again and more settled but I couldn't help but wonder if he been hurting them behind my back. I'll never know, I was just glad he was out of our lives and I wished I'd never met him. I'd been on my own for over a year when Raymond started to walk and was getting into everything. I seemed to be managing okay. One particular day I was on my way to Mum's when a van pulled up alongside me, *not someone else wanting directions, why can't they get maps?* I thought to myself. As I turned, the man said "Hello Tina." Talk about a blast from the past! It was Keith, bloody hell I used to babysit his son years ago. I hadn't seen him in over four years. We had a little chat, "How you doing it's been a long time," that sort of thing. Then he wanted to know if I was with someone. I almost said yes but something told me to say no. We exchanged numbers and he went on his way delivering in the area. A couple of days later, he rang me and we talked about the old times and what he'd been up to. It seemed he divorced his wife and moved out of the area. Then he met wife number two. He had two boys with her but they had just split up. She had moved back to her mother's and taken the boys with her. He asked how my family was and I told him they were just fine. Just before he went, he wanted to know if he could come round to see me next time he was in the area. I had to refuse, *I couldn't trust another man* but if he wanted to meet me in public I would consider that. He refused because you can't talk about private things. I hope it wasn't advice he wanted, I'm no Margery Proops. What private things did we need to talk about? I told him, we were just two old friends catching up. I became very weary so I decided to leave it to phone calls for a while. It could have been me being paranoid but, with my track record with men and relationships, I was wondering if there was something wrong with me? I can honestly say I loved them but I wasn't in love with them, was I missing something? I don't know. Keith phoned me every night for two weeks. It was small talk really, how you doing, how was your day? And so on. Then one night out of the blue, I asked him to come round if he wasn't busy. The next day I busied myself cleaning it wasn't my usual cleaning day so why was I doing it? He was only a friend, or was he? Did I want more from him or was it the other way round? It was eight o'clock, the kids were fed, watered, bathed and in bed, and I sat there waiting. I wondered if I'd done a wise thing inviting him round, was I hoping to find something that wasn't there? He eventually turned up and, as we sat chatting he told me about the place he lived and how peaceful it was. I had no idea he'd moved. I thought he still lived in the area. the more he told me the more I liked the sound of the place and it was ideal for bringing up children. It sounded like the place I originated from, plenty of room for the kids to run around in but no sea.

CHAPTER 8
THE CHILDREN

By the early part of 1981, Keith and I were in a relationship. Unlike the other two he stayed most of the week. The kids and I were spending the weekends with him so we could see his home. Things seemed different with him, maybe because I knew him before. He picked us up on the Friday evening, I made sure the kids were fed as it was about an hour's drive. So by the time we arrived there it would be getting dark so all I had to do was to put them to bed. After they were settled, we had a trip down memory lane. It was so relaxing and peaceful, just to sit and talk. His home used to be a working cottage where a farm hand and his family once lived and, by the looks of it, nothing had changed. It had three bedrooms and in the living room. There was a parkray fire; the kitchen was quite large with plenty of cupboard space and an old wood burner *wow*. There was an entrance near the back door and, as you went through it, there was the bathroom. I found it quite strange that it was downstairs and especially through the kitchen. I could see myself living there but I didn't let on to Keith. In the morning, I sorted the kids out and got them ready so he could take us on a guided tour of .the village. It took about twenty minutes for us to walk around it. There were twenty five houses in his street and just across the road from his cottage was a small shop come post office. At one end of the street there was a church and at the other end there was a pub. I had to laugh, I couldn't help myself. When I said to him, "Well you'll have somewhere to sin and somewhere to confess your sins." He couldn't stop laughing for quite a while. As we walked back to his place, a few of the neighbours stopped to speak to him. I thought *the nosy gits, they only want to find out who I was.* Keith spoke to them but didn't introduce me; I think he was waiting to see what I thought of the place. When we got back, we let the kids play in the back garden as it was quite mild for the time of year *oh my God!* The size of it! It was at least sixty foot long, thirty feet wide and all grass. The kids loved it. The weekend soon came to an end and I didn't want to go back home to my demons but I had to wait for him to ask me.

This was the place, new memories could be made and good ones too I hoped. On the way back, Keith wanted to know what I thought of the place. I told him how nice it was and how the kids loved it. He didn't say a word. I don't know what he expected me to say. Things carried on as they did with him coming to me in the week and I went to his with the kids at the weekends. One weekend he asked me again what I thought of the place. I told him exactly what I told him before, " I like the place and it is ideal for bringing up the kids; plenty of fresh air and no crime." He then asked me if I'd like to move in with him. *About bloody time.* Without hesitation he got a yes but I needed to get things sorted out back home. I had to tell Mum and Henry and give the council a month's notice. That night we made a list of things I needed to take with me and the things I could sell. On the list Keith put the kids' beds for sale. I told him to get rid of the ones he already had as I'd be bringing them with me. We had a bit of a disagreement over it until I explained that Henry had made them with his own two hands, and if I sold them, I would feel as though I'd betraying him or insulting him after everything he'd done for me in the past. Keith understood and was okay with it.

Because we'd been at Keith's for the weekend I'd only left enough milk for a cuppa for when I got home. As soon as I could Monday morning, I went to the local shop to get milk and a few other bits that I needed. The next thing I knew, Lew was approaching me. I started to shiver with fear, I asked him "What the hell do you want?" The sick bastard only wanted to see my children! I told him to go away and told him he lost his rights to be called granddad years ago. That caused a scene outside the shop. He said, "I am your father so that makes me their granddad, I have all the rights to see the kids." Quite a few people passing agreed with him, but I wondered if they would if they knew he molested me as a child? I said to them, "Mind your own business you don't know me and you don't know what's happened." Then I turned to him and said, "While I am still walking and breathing, you will never have anything to do with us. By this time the fear had subsided and turned to anger. I walked into the shop, got my bits and by the time I'd paid for them and left he had gone. I put the incident with him at the back of my mind. I needed to tell Mum about Keith asking me to move in with him. As soon as possible, I went round to Mum's and told her what I was doing. They wanted to know if I was sure about it and what made me decide to do it. I stopped and thought for a minute. I couldn't tell them the truth about the demons that followed me around the place and I still couldn't tell her what Lew had done to me. I don't know if I was trying to protect Mum or I didn't want to admit I let it happen. Even now I feel dirty and I kept asking myself, "could I have stopped it?" I could never get the right answers and I don't think I ever will. If ever the topic of conversation cropped up on any case of child molestation, I would always hear the same thing, "They were only children, what could they do?" I listened to the conversations, hoping to get answers for myself but I never did and I still don't feel any better in myself either. I told Mum that it would be a fresh start being in the countryside and the fresh air would do the kids the world of good. Not only that, it would be somewhere for them to come even if it was for just a day out. I hoped they couldn't tell it was only a part truth so the rest of the day Henry played hide and seek with the kids and me and Mum sat chatting. I could tell there was something bothering Mum. I asked her and she just gave me a false smile and said, "Everything is fine. " I could tell that it wasn't but I had to leave before it got dark so I couldn't push the subject.

I got the kids settled down and just sat on my own looking around the house, wondering if I'd made the right decision. There was no answer to it; I just needed to take my mind off it and relax, *how was I going to do that I asked myself.* Then I remembered Henry gave me cassette tape of classical music. I wasn't really into music, especially classical, but I put it on, switched off the main lights and put the lamp on. I laid on the couch listening to what I thought was rubbish when all of a sudden I could feel the tension floating away and a sense of ease coming over me. I must have drifted off when all of a sudden I woke with a start and the feeling that someone else was in the room with me. I must have been dreaming, no one else was there but no matter what I did I couldn't get rid of that feeling. I went from room to room looking but no one was there. I started talking to myself, "Don't be silly all the windows and doors are locked, no one can get in." But the feeling was so over whelming that I couldn't sleep. I moved Raymond into Chantelle's room and sat with them all night. What was causing this? Could it have been the music or was it the demons trying to get back in? I didn't know. I couldn't wait to move after that. I thought I might just be able to lead a normal life. I'd had enough of looking over my shoulders every time I went out. It was something I'd not stopped doing since that day I jumped out of the window. I kept looking to see just in case Lew was anywhere about, even though I'd not seen him since they divorced in the early part of nineteen seventy four, until that day, when he approached me at the shop. The fear and self loathing was embedded in me and then there was Alan and Dan. Would they try to get their kids? Now my question was answered, "Yes, it was the right choice to move." The next day despite a lack of sleep, I started to write cards to put into the local shop windows. I needed to get rid of quite a lot of items so I went to all the shops in the area there were quite a few of them. It wasn't long before the phone started to ring and everything was sold. I rang Keith and told him I was handing my keys back to the council earlier than first thought, gave him a date so he could arrange time off work and get a van. It was weird going around the almost bare rooms. I had to borrow a chair to sit on, *I didn't think about somewhere to park my bum when I was selling everything.* In the end Mum came to the rescue. She also told me I could stay with them as it would give them the chance to see their grand kids before I went. She didn't know when she'd see them again.

On the day of the move, Mum had the kids and I made sure I was at my house early. When I walked into the house, an eerie feeling came over me and the place was stone cold. It could have been because it had been closed up for a few days and my mind was playing tricks on me. I opened all the windows and doors but nothing took that feeling away so I decided to wait outside. It felt like hours had passed before Keith turned up. I was so relieved to see him but I couldn't tell him about the feeling I had or I thought there was something wrong with the house; would he believe me or would he think I was going mad? *I even thought that I was going mad myself at one point.* Keith brought a mate to help him *thank God.* I was dubious about going back in there but I couldn't leave everything for the boys to do. When it was all loaded, the boys took the van back to unload it and then Keith said he would be back for us later on. After they had driven off, a sense of dread came over me. Would he come back for us or was this a sick joke he was playing? After I had the feeling someone else was in the house, I was imagining all sorts of things it was my imagination running wild. Keith came back a few hours later; it was just me thinking the worst. After having a cuppa with Mum and Henry, it was time for us to leave. They gave the kids a long cuddle, "Until we see you again" Mum said to them. By the time we got to the village, just outside of Leighton Buzzard, the kids were tired. Mum had fed them so it was a case of PJ's and off to bed. The rest of the evening was relaxation time but I couldn't. There was still too much going on in my head. Had I made the right move? Was this going to work? Why was I having those feelings back at the other house and would I get on with the neighbours? All this stuff was going round in my head and I kept going from one thing to another, trying to solve them.

I wasn't unduly bothered about the neighbours and only time would tell, they would either like me or not at the end of the day it was up to them. Before I knew it, my bed was calling. I wasn't sure if I'd be able to sleep; I was unsettled and tossed and turned most of the night. Maybe it was because there was so much to do, trying to make the place look like a home and not a pig sty, or maybe because this was a major step for me and I was apprehensive. One thing I can say about Keith, he was clueless about cleaning and organising things, *but that goes for most men women do all the cleaning.* Then there was the smell, the smell of a man living on his own for so long. The next morning, I sorted the kids out and then I started a major cleanup campaign. I started with the bedrooms, curtains, nets, and put the bedding in the wash. There were cobwebs everywhere; the spiders were spoilt for choice. I always thought it was foggy outside but hell no, it was dirty windows! I was a woman on a mission, everything was done by lunchtime and I had plenty of time to play ball and other games with the kids. I still had the downstairs to do but that would take some time. There were newspapers and letters all over the place and boxes to be unpacked. I gathered up all the newspapers, put them outside the back door, then I put all his letters on the table. What a difference that made! By the time I'd finished, the place even smelt clean. It was now four thirty and I hadn't started the dinner so it was something quick and easy just for tonight. When Keith came home, the first thing he noticed was that his newspapers weren't there. He started balling and shouting, *you would have thought I'd committed murder!* I told him where they were so he went to retrieve them and took them upstairs to his wardrobe *God knows why?* After seeing that display of manhood, I'd wondered if I'd done the right thing, what could I do now? Then, I thought maybe he'd had a bad day at work. If that was the case, he'd have to learn to leave work at work at not bring it home with him. After he had calmed down and had his dinner, he noticed that the house looked and smelt clean. By now I had to bath and get the kids ready for bed then we both settled down for the night. It was my time to relax. I decided to bring up the way he came home from work and put him straight, "We are not there for you to take your anger on," I told him. He agreed he was in the wrong and should never have reacted like that he said, "I'll make it up to you." He said.

My birthday was coming up. I'd be twenty one and to make

it up to me, he was going to throw me a party. He asked me if I'd go into town and get the invitations so we could get them out into the post and every week we'd get other bits and pieces. On the day, I got the decorations up and the food ready. By now I was calling Henry Dad. He told us we didn't have to but we all wanted to; he earned the title more than Lew ever did. Henry might not have been our biological dad but he was the nearest thing to one we'd ever have. He seemed to understand us and knew where we were coming from. I didn't know Keith had invited them *bless him,* so while he was out getting the last minute bits there was a knock at the door, to my surprise it was them. They heard me shouting and wanted to know who I was shouting at. They thought I was either having an argument with Keith or having a break down, which wouldn't have been surprising after what I'd been through with Lew, Andy, Dan and Alan. I explained to them it was Ethel a friendly ghost who kept taking things. I was shouting at her to put the bloody things back. I didn't know which was worse, the fact I was talking to a ghost or Mum thinking I was having a breakdown. The colour drained from Mum's face, I think it was shock, because she thought I'd lost the plot. After the shock had worn off, it wasn't too long before the guests started to arrive. The whole village was invited. Keith thought it would be the best way for me to met them all. There was just one man he didn't invite; Phillip. He was the village trouble maker. Any trouble and he would be right in the middle of it so Keith didn't want to take the chance *quite sensible of him.* I was introduced to everyone. They all seemed nice, apart from one lady named Sara; she was right up herself and looked down on some of the guests. I knew she'd be trouble. I never said anything, I just kept a beady eye on her. After all the introductions had been done, the party went into full swing and everyone looked to be enjoying themselves when I heard shouting and a voice I didn't recognise. As I walked into the room where the shouting was coming from, a man whom I didn't know was stood there I asked him who he was. He said "Phillip." He wanted to know why he was the only one not invited. When I told him he was like a baby who'd lost his dummy I asked him to leave, he flew into a rage. Mum and Dad tried to stay out of the way as some of the guests tried to get him out but he managed to push them. Then he picked up a chair and threw it! By now my blood was at boiling point, *how dare he gate crash my party and ruin it?* I managed to jump on his back but he threw me across the room. *He wasn't going to get the best of me*, so I mustered all my strength and jumped on his back again. This time he went flying onto the floor, Keith and the others managed to get him out. *It took a woman to do a man's job*. When he got outside, he realised it was me *a mere woman* who knocked him to the floor. His male pride must have been hurt so he got hold of me and started to hit me! Sara's husband Clive saw what he was doing and tried to get him off me. When he did, Phillip did no more than to smash his face into a brick wall; there was blood everywhere. Meanwhile, someone had rung the police and, by the time they arrived, it was all over. Phillip was arrested on various counts and poor Clive was rushed to hospital with severe injuries to his face. We all gave our statements and went home, apart from Keith's mate Paul who stayed behind to help us with the cleaning up *bless him*. I told Mum and Dad to go to bed and we'd sort the cleaning out. By the time we'd finished, it was the early hours. We tried to get a few hours sleep before the kids woke up luckily enough they slept through the drama. When we were all up, I noticed Mum was covered in bruises. I wanted to know how she got them but she didn't know, she kept out of the way when it kicked off and Dad didn't have a mark on him at all *how lucky was he?* After breakfast; I went round to Sara's to see how Clive was doing. She'd only just got back from the hospital and told me Clive had to have an operation on his face. Phillip had literally smashed his face in so it had to be rebuilt and have pins put in to hold some of the parts into place. Then, she blamed me saying, "If you would have invited Phillip to your party, then this wouldn't have happened." I replied "If he hadn't gate crashed it then things would have been different." It was one of those things we would never agree on. After I left her, I went to see the other guests to make sure they were all right. When I got back, I told Keith no more parties. After that memorable night, things went on as normal. There was something missing but I couldn't put my finger on it. Everything was still the same; Keith went to work and I did the usual mundane things I'd done for years. It had been a long time since I first had feelings like this, something was missing in my life, I couldn't put my finger on it. I knew it couldn't be the relationship because they had all been different. Then, I thought maybe it was losing Charlotte all those years ago but it wasn't that either. I couldn't talk to Keith about how I was feeling in case he thought I wasn't happy with him. As the months went on, the feelings never went away. They were getting worse and, I still couldn't put a finger on what was missing. By the time Christmas came I was pregnant again. It was due in the summer and I was dreading telling Keith because we agreed we wouldn't have any until we were more settled. When I did tell him, he was straight on the phone to his mother and told her. I was not happy he did that I wanted to wait before telling anyone. Then he phoned my Mum and told her which caused an argument because I wanted to be the one to tell her and Dad when the time was right but he took that decision out of my hands. I made sure every day was filled with fun things for the kids to do while he was at work but I still had my doubts about whether I'd made the right choice in moving. But I was pregnant with my third so I'd have to make the best of it and make this relationship last if only for the kid's sake. Chantelle and Raymond were now calling Keith Daddy and it wouldn't be fair on them. They already had enough upset in their little lives with Dan, the move and being away from their Nan and Granddad. Life still had to go on and I had to make the best of it.

The next door neighbour was a sweet old lady; she would pop in to see if I needed anything or just to have a chat and a cuppa. Her name was Rosetta but the kids called her Rose. I though Rosetta was Italian or Spanish with a name like that but she was born here in England. It happened her father was in the services and was stationed in Italy. While he was there, he fell in love with the name Rosetta. Rose had two sons and a daughter who were still living at home with her. We never really saw them, only the backs of their heads as they were walking down the street. She came round one day really upset and said, "We need to talk" *Bloody hell not a Margery Proops moment?* She sat down and I made us a cuppa. She was just about to say something when the floodgates opened. Through her tears, I could make out the odd word and managed to work out that Keith and gone to see her to tell her to stay away from us, why would he tell her that? He had no reason or so I thought.

Apparently, he came home from work one day, found his ex wife in bed with her eldest son and ended up throwing them both out. Now I knew what caused the split between them, *thank God it wasn't a Margery Proops moment.* Keith was scared that history would repeat its self. For him to think that it proved to me that he had no trust in me. It was like I had a sign on my head saying, "not to be trusted." How could I live like this and how could he compare me to his ex? We were nothing alike; I had to quickly sort it out before he stopped all my visitors. I waited till he came home and the kids were in bed, then I asked him how his marriage broke up. He told me exactly what Rose had done except he left the bit out about it being Rose's son, then I asked him "What gives you the right to say what visitors I have?" Then, he told me it was her son. He wanted to know how I found out so I told him that I'd gone round to see her but she didn't invite me in so I asked her, "is there a problem?" and it was then she told me what he had said to her. I told Keith that if he wanted our relationship to last, then he'd better stop dictating who I could and couldn't see anymore of this and I'd be gone. He hated the fact I'd given him an ultimatum and now he knew I wouldn't be controlled by him. Too many men in my past had tried; I didn't need him to as well. He was told that if he couldn't trust me, it was pointless us being together and that he also needed to apologise to Rose, it wasn't her fault that her son slept with his ex wife. He refused to do that, so the next time we were out together and we saw Rose, I apologised to her in front of him. That didn't please him at all but I didn't give a dam. I might have lived with him, but he certainly wasn't my owner, no man would own me, even if I was married to them. It was only a matter of weeks before I was due and it was the wrong time to go upsetting folks. Sooner or later we would need their help with Chantelle and Raymond unless he had no intensions of coming to the hospital *or were they suppose to look after themselves?* It made him think about it, he hated being in the wrong *but what man likes to be?* Things got back to almost normal. There were a few chinks that needed ironing out but I'd get there in the end.

The middle of July 1982, it seemed hotter than previous years. We were sat in the garden, watching the kids playing, when all of a sudden I felt wet. When I looked down, I realised my waters had broke but I wasn't in labour yet. Keith rang the hospital and explained to them. They advised him to give me an hour and, if the labour pains hadn't started to take me in. Less than an hour later the pains kicked in. Keith got Rose to have the kids. As we drove the pains stopped. He was just about to turn round when I got the urge to push. He must have broken all speed records to get me there before I pushed and, as we pulled up there was a nurse just about to go on duty. He shouted at her and told her the baby was on its way. She rushed to get a wheel chair and took me straight to the delivery room. As soon as they got me onto the bed to check me out the baby had come. Another beautiful daughter! Seven pounds thirteen ounces. Because she came so quickly, *she must have been in one hell of a rush to see the outside world,* they kept me in overnight just to make sure everything was fine. Chantelle was like an old mother hen, trying to help *bless her.* We decided to name her Naomi. It was a matter of days before my twenty second birthday I made sure Keith was not thinking about a party for me. Over the next three years, I had another two children; Terry and Katie. After Katie was born, we decided not to have anymore and it was also about time we got married. Well, Keith thought it was time I wasn't sure; I was still looking for that something that was still missing in my life. I spoke to Rose about it and she seemed to think it was because I wasn't married. She had a point it could have been. I agreed with her. Just maybe she was right.

CHAPTER 9
MY FIRST MARRIAGE

The day of my wedding was almost here and Keith told me everything was ready for it; all I had to do was to make sure I was at the registry office. I would have loved the traditional white wedding with it being my first but with Keith being a divorcee we couldn't be married in church, *never mind we can't have it all.* On the day, I put on a dress he'd bought me. It was nice, however, it wasn't me. We asked Rose if she'd be kind enough to have the kids, then the taxi arrived for me I wasn't expecting a fanfare on my arrival, however, I was expecting a little more than the witnesses being pulled off the street and a few drinks in the local pub. I should have known things weren't quite right, but I put it down to having five kids and a wedding on the cheap. At least I had a real wedding ring but Keith didn't want a ring. He told me he couldn't wear one because of his job and like an idiot, I believed him. He hadn't done anything or said anything for me to doubt him but something was bugging me. The next day, I tried to settle down to married life but it wasn't any different to how it was before the wedding. The only difference was I had a ring on my finger but something was still missing and I still didn't know what it was, it was just a feeling I couldn't shake off. *I'd made my bed and now I'd have to lie on it.* I had no choice but to carry on the best way I could. Three months later and still things didn't feel right. I couldn't put my finger on it even the neighbours seemed distant. I told Keith about it and all he said was, "It's all in your mind, nothing has changed."

A few weeks later, there was a knock at the door. When I answered it, I was shocked to see someone from the N.S.P.C.C stood there. At first I thought they were collecting for their charity but they soon made it clear it was me they had come to see. I invited them in and it was then they told me they'd received a phone call telling them I was locking the kids in the bedroom and not giving them enough to eat. The icing on the cake I was that I was also beating them. I had to laugh! Just before they knocked, I'd just finished putting the shopping away. They wanted to check the house; I had nothing to hide so I told them to be my guest. First, they wanted to look downstairs. The kid's toys were all over the place so least they couldn't say they had no toys to play with. Then, on to the kitchen where they checked all the cupboards. As they did, a tin fell out of one of them *shame it didn't hit them on the head* and then they had the cheek to check the fridge. When they got up stairs, they were looking at the bedroom doors and then had audacity to ask me where the bolts were. Anyone with any intelligence could see there were no marks or holes on the doors or frames so how the hell could there have been any bolts fitted on them? The next thing was they wanted to check the children. The older ones got undressed down to their underwear and I undressed the younger ones, *how humiliating especially for the older kids.* There wasn't a single bruise on any of them so I told them to get the hell out of my house. That evening, when Keith came home, I asked him, "Which one of your so called friends would do something like that?" He said, "Stop being paranoid, it couldn't have been any of them." He then asked me, "Are you sure it wasn't the doctor or the health visitor?" I told him not to be so bloody stupid, "I haven't seen them in a while and the last time they saw the kids there was nothing on them. They were all healthy so that just leaves the people that knew us. Open your eyes and see what's going on in front of them." With that, we had one almighty row and he called me a fucking bitch, a stupid cow and a few other choice words in front of the kids. *Why had I let myself in for another abusive man?* I put the kids upstairs then I put him straight, "I am your wife and you need to show some respect. In future, you don't do that in front of the kids because if you do then I will have to think whether this marriage will work." He got up to hit me, he thought I was going to run. I'd had enough abuse over the years so I stood there and showed him I wasn't running away. He just left the house. He was gone for hours and when he returned I was on my way up to bed. I had to laugh. He wanted to know where his dinner was; I told him to look in the bin and if he wanted something he'd have to make it himself. He grabbed my arm and pulled me back and said, "You're my wife and you have to do my meals." I saw red. If I would have got away with murder then I would have killed him. I told him that too and reminded him I was his wife, not his bloody servant. Then I went to bed.

The following day he did nothing but apologise but he was just like all the other men I'd known; a bully. At least I was prepared this time because of the others. He wouldn't get a chance to do it again. As the year went on he'd changed; he was never at home, always out with his friends, friends I'd never met or heard him speak about. Then he changed his job, the job, he loved. I couldn't get my head around that, *why change a job he loved so much, did he have an argument with the boss or one of his work mates, did he threaten anyone?* It just didn't make any sense at all; I wanted to know why he changed his job. He told me he was bored with it. There was something more to it; you don't just get bored with a job you love.

Nothing was making any sense to me but I had other things to worry about; five children and who would want them taken off me? I had an idea but I couldn't prove it. I let it be known I knew who it was and if there was another knock at my door from the N.S.P.C.C then I would sue for defamation of character. For the time being I'd keep the person's name to myself. Keith hadn't been in his new job as a taxi driver for long when he decided to change his hours from days to nights because he could earn more money. I wasn't happy about it because as he was getting in, I was getting up, so much for married life! I would have been better on my own. This was my life now, stuck at home with five kids, no friends and no one I could turn to. I'd been through worse and come through it so I could do it again. Although it was slightly different this time; I had the kids to keep me busy and stop me from returning to my past, the place I never wanted to visit again if I could help it. It was coming up to our anniversary; I was hoping that we'd do something special that didn't include the kids. We never had any time together, all he was interested in was work, work and work. To try to make things good, I bought him a beautiful card and a few gifts. It wasn't a lot but I made an effort. The day of our anniversary was upon us and, to make more of an effort, I cooked him his favourite breakfast a full English. When he got up he wasn't hungry *I'd never known a man refuse a full English breakfast.* Then he told me he'd been offered an extra shift at work. I was now beginning to get suspicious. After he had left the house, I rang the taxi firm to speak to him and they told me he wouldn't be in until later. So I asked about some other dates he told me he was working and half of them he wasn't there. I didn't know what to do; say something to him or leave it and see if I could find out what he was up to? Where would I start? Who could I trust? I decided to do nothing and hoped he'd make a mistake. Because I was going to be on my own at night, I persuaded him to get me a C.B radio just for the company. At least I'd have people to chat to. He set it up for me but I just stood and stared at it. I had no idea what to do or what to say so he gave me a quick lesson. Anything I didn't catch I'd have to pick up myself. It didn't take me long and, before I knew it, I was chatting away mostly to lorry drivers. There were a lot of interesting people out there! On the odd occasion, Keith would come on and chat. Because I was a voice at the end of a mic, the drivers found it easy to talk to me and get stuff off their minds whether it be their wives, jobs or just family in general, *bloody hell now I've turned into Margery Proops*. I had a couple of handles on air Gold Label if it was for general chat and Fine Lady cut short to F.L if it was for a Margery Proops moment.

One particular night has stuck in my mind all these years. It was after I had put the kids to bed and Keith had gone to work. I was sat waiting for anyone to come on air then a man came on and told me he was unsure what to do. His problem was one of his mates was having an affair and he was married with kids, he didn't know whether to say something to him or leave him to his own devices. The only advice I could give him was to go with what his heart was saying and not his head. This man played on my mind all night; had I given him the right advice? Was there something more I could have said? All I could do was to wait until I went on air again and see if he came back on to tell me what he decided to do. I must have drifted off; I woke up a few hours later and Keith was beside me, *what he was doing home?* He had come home earlier than normal to get a few hours kip because he was covering for one of the drivers on the day shift. I hadn't been up long before he got up and was out of the door. Although the C.B was meant to be used at night, I thought I'd switch it on, the kids were still in bed so I didn't see the harm, as I listened I had to chuckle to myself at some of the things the truckers were coming out with. Then, all of a sudden, a voice came on calling for F.L. I was unsure whether to answer it in case Keith came back; he sometimes popped in for a quick cuppa if he was dropping off in the area. I thought sod it, someone needs me. As I answered it, I recognised the voice from the previous night it was Road Runner. I just made small talk with him, "How are you? Are you at work?" All he was doing was seeing if I was okay and if I'd had a good night's sleep. I said "I am fine and I slept like a baby." I thought it was a bit odd he would ask me that but I guess he was just being thoughtful. I didn't want to chat for too long in case Keith popped in and I also had things to be getting on with before the kids got up. I left the C.B on when I heard Road Runner calling for another driver "Road Rocket." I'd never heard this handle before so I assumed he was new on air. As he replied to Road Runner I listened and the voice seemed familiar, I changed the channel so I could hear better, and as I listened, it became clear Road Rocket was having an affair. I was just about to change the channel again when Road Runner asked if he'd come clean to his wife. I was shocked when he referred to his wife as a "slapper" and "she is only good for one thing and "it is none of your business". Road Rocket's voice still seemed familiar but I couldn't put my finger on it. I stopped what I was doing and listened carefully to the conversation. Road Runner was asking him how his kids would feel *what a caring man* and how it wasn't fair on them. Road Rocket replied that he only had interest one of them and that was his daughter; the other two were mistakes. I thought to myself *what a pig,* it made no difference if they were mistakes or not, at the end of the day they were still his children. I still couldn't work out where I'd heard that voice before and there was nothing in it that gave me a clue. I had to switch off as the kids were getting up. Just as they were finishing their breakfast, Keith walked in and he switched on the C.B, something he didn't usually do then. I heard Road Runner give a call for Road Rocket. There was no reply then, all of a sudden, Keith switched it off and told me he had to go out. As soon as I heard him drive off, I switched it back on and flicked through the channels until I found what I was looking for. As I was flicking, I was wondering why he'd gone out in such a hurry. I then heard the call for Road Rocket or was I being paranoid? I was just about to switch off when Road Runner, said "If you don't tell your wife then I'd have no choice but to tell her myself." He replied by saying, "Do your worst! My Mrs. wouldn't believe you." Then came the answers I was looking for; *C.B's are great for spying and finding out things*. Road Runner told him that it wouldn't be fair on Tina, Terry and Katie and he should take his responsibilities seriously. Road Rocket just laughed and said, "If I come clean about everything, Tina will walk out, take the children and there was no way I am going to lose Naomi. How much do you expect me to tell her? This is not my first, there have been others, at least three over the last five years and the silly cow had no idea about any of them. She believed everything I told her." What a good job he had a C. B in his car, how stupid of him to not to think that I could be listening. As I sat listening to them, it occurred to me what would be the odds of someone with my name and having three children with the same names? It then hit me like a ton of hot bricks: I was me the wife, the silly cow believed everything he told me, *he wasn't wrong on that one*, but no more. As for only being interested in only one child, when he had three of his own and two he took on as his, I couldn't believe what I was hearing I had to switch off.

I needed time to think, is this the end or could we get past it ? Deep down, I knew our marriage was over. I had to think of the children and not myself. What was the next step and how should I go about it? He was out most of the day. Considering he was supposed to be on nights, I had to assume he was at hers whoever she was so he was obviously getting his sleep there. He told me he had to work because one of the drivers was off sick what a fucking liar! I saw this particular driver dropping off one of my neighbours. I went through the day with it eating away at me, pretending everything was fine in front of the kid., He was out most of the night continuing which ever lie was suitable for him. Assuming he'd be home that night it would have been too late to confront him and I wasn't in the mood for an argument so I had to stew all night. He did finally come home *oh lucky me*. The next morning, he was up and out before I could say anything to him *the bastard* so I went around the house putting his belongings into a bag and then I phoned him to come home straight away. It was over between us and it wasn't something I was going to say over the phone, I needed to do it face to face so he knew there was no coming back. Whatever he said to me made no difference. As he walked through the door, I could see by his face he was in a bad mood but I couldn't let that stop me. He wanted to know what the emergency was. I showed him his bags and said, "It's over." He had the audacity to ask, "Why?" "I heard everything you said, so the silly cow will believe everything I say and this is not my first. I've had three over the last five years." He tried telling me it was a game he was playing with his mate because he knew I was listening, what a liar! Did he think I came over on the last banana boat? Then he went on to say, "It's only you and the children I want." Then I hit him with it "Don't you mean Naomi? She's the only one you want. Let me tell you now you, will never get

161

any of the children so, if I was you, I'd pick up my things and get out and don't bother coming back." He picked up his things and walked out of the door. Rose saw him leaving with his bags in tow and came round to see if everything was alright and so did some of the other neighbours. I explained to them what had been going on and after all that had been said and done, I'd told him to leave. Then it hit me like a wrecking ball; I was on my own with five kids stuck in a village where everybody was too busy putting their noses into things that didn't concern them. The nearest town was a mile and a quarter away with one bus a week on a Tuesday so it was impossible for me to do my shopping with five kids in tow. I couldn't afford a taxi and there wasn't one with enough seats for us all. The neighbours were at work and weekends they had theirs to do with their families. I wouldn't ask Rose to have the kids she had her own family and she wasn't getting any younger. I had a lot of thinking to do. What was my next step?

CHAPTER 10
THE DIVORCE

The next day, I made an appointment with a solicitor to get advice. The first thing he told me to do was to get the house put into my name because he had the right to come in and evict me with or without the kids. We didn't have a joint bank account so that wasn't a problem. As soon as got home, I rang the council to make an appointment about getting the house transferred into my name. I was worried about whether or not I could cope on my own with the five kids. I spent the rest of the day making sure the kids were happy. They kept asking when Dad was coming home but he wasn't coming home, and I had to find a way of telling them so that they'd understand. No matter what I thought of, nothing sounded right so I decided not to say anything to them and leave it up him to explain if he ever saw them again.

The following day I had my appointment at the council. As I sat there a feeling of uneasiness came over me. I put It down to the situation I was in. I was called into an office where a woman was sat. She wasn't very nice. I tried to explain the position to her but she wouldn't listen to me so, I refused to talk to her anymore and asked if there was anyone else I could talk to. She went and got her supervisor who asked me what the problem was. I explained to her about the other woman and how she wouldn't listen to me so the supervisor took over and again I had to explain the predicament I was in. Then the supervisor hit me with a bomb shell; the council was taking us to court to get an eviction notice because Keith hadn't paid any rent for quite a while. There were arrears of over two thousand pounds and, because the house was in joint names, I was also liable. I told her that the house wasn't in joint names, only his and I hadn't signed anything. Then she showed me the tenancy agreement. My name was on it but it wasn't my signature. I gave her a sample of mine to prove I hadn't signed it and she was happy that I hadn't put my name to it. She informed the police and they had to investigate. Apparently Keith got his new girlfriend to sign it on my behalf without my knowledge and that proved I was no longer liable for the arrears. I was able to keep the house which I was more than relieved about. The next thing I had to do was to make an appointment for the Department of Social Security to claim housing benefits so my rent could be paid. Then I had to find a solicitor and apply for legal aid to get a divorce on the grounds of adultery. When Keith found out it was for adultery, he was furious! He thought it was going to be on the grounds the marriage wasn't working out, *he must be so thick?* Of course it wasn't working out he was committing adultery! We never discussed a divorce and, even if we had, I would still have gone through with it. He thought that I'd sit back and let him carry on with his harlots *how mistaken was he?* Before the divorce could go ahead, there was the custody of the children to sort out. The solicitor applied to the courts for a date for the hearing. In the meantime, Keith came to see me about access to see the kids. After a heated conversation we agreed on every Saturday at two o'clock. He did mention that it would be only his three and that one week he would take two together and the other week and the other one he would take on his next visit. We did agree that it would only be his biological kids. The week passed the same as any other week, Saturday was here and I made sure the two were dressed smartly. I didn't tell them they were going out with their Dad I thought it would be a nice surprise for them. Two o'clock sharp he turned up and, when I answered the door, I noticed a woman in the car. I didn't say anything at that time. I didn't want or need an argument especially in front of the kids. As I went to call the kids, it was then he told me he was only taking Naomi and the other two would have to wait until the following weekend. I was so angry with him but what could I do? I couldn't force him to take the others. Luckily, the solicitor told me to keep a record of events. I didn't understand why he was telling me to do that at the time, although he did try to explain it all to me.

It went on for months until one day he picked Naomi up and didn't return her at five o'clock as we agreed. He brought her back an hour later and she seemed to be a lot happier on this trip more so than on previous outings with her Dad. I soon found out why. He passed me a bag and in it was a new dress, shoes and a few other bits, I made sure she said, "Thank you," and left it at that. I told the other two that Dad couldn't afford to take them all out together, how could I tell them that Naomi was his favourite? After I'd settled them down for the night, I sat there thinking was he playing some sort of game or was he just doing the father thing? I took the things out of the bag to put them away. The price tags were still on them so I had a look. He'd spent almost one hundred pounds on her and got it all from B.H.S. The following Saturday soon came around, I got Terry and Katie ready for him and mentioned that they needed new shoes. He moaned about it but agreed to get them some. As the day went on, I couldn't stop thinking if he'd get theirs from the same shop or not. He brought them back on time, bags in hand. Their shoes were from a discount shoe shop and their clothes were from a discount clothes shop. I waited until I put them to bed then I calculated how much he'd spent on them both; it was about fifty pounds each. I found that despicable. He should have spent the same on the three of them, not more on one and less on the others. They were his kids and he should treat them all the same. It played on my mind all week, how could he treat his children so differently? The next time I saw him I'd have to have it out with him. He was running late picking Naomi up so I didn't get the opportunity, but I would when he brought her back. The day dragged and I tried to occupy my mind on other things but I couldn't, I was so livid. It was getting close to the time they were due back and I was looking out of the window for them to return. Then, I saw him drive up and went to the door to meet them. Naomi got out of the car and stood there crying. Keith didn't bother to get out. I was just about to ask him what the problem was when he drove off, the bastard couldn't be bothered to tell me what happened to upset her. I asked her if she had a nice time and she started to cry again. She told me she didn't want to go and live with him and that woman. I was totally confused. I never said to her she was going to live with her Dad. Then, she explained that the woman had told her that she was going to live with them and she was going to be her new Mum. I couldn't believe what she had just told me! It took me ages to calm her down and reassure her that wouldn't happen, that the woman would never be her Mum and that she had no right in saying that to her. I phoned Keith and told him I needed to see him on his own and it was concerning the children. I could hear the other woman in the background, telling him he wasn't going anywhere without her. I told him to tell her to shut her mouth and it had nothing to do with her. I wanted to talk to him without her then I would. I put the phone down and waited to see what would happen, if anything. Two hours later he was knocking so I let him in. As soon as Naomi saw him she ran and hid, the poor soul thought he'd come back for her. I thought it best to leave her until he'd gone. He wanted to know what was so important that it couldn't wait until next weekend. He was told that if he wanted to see his kids then he had to do it without his new girlfriend and she had nothing to do with them. As for her being their new Mum, in her dreams. They only had one Mum and one Mum only that was me. He tried to argue the fact but I told him straight, "If she continues to see the children then I would have no option but to stop his visits until it went to court and then we'll let the court decide." He didn't have much of a choice but to agree to my terms. What I didn't know was the devious bastard was trying to get custody of Naomi *I didn't find out until we went to court*. After he had left, Naomi came out and played as though nothing was wrong. First thing Monday morning I was straight on the phone to my solicitor and told him everything. He told me the hearing would be in five weeks and there was a letter on its way to me.

The five weeks soon passed and it was time for the hearing, I asked Rose if she'd mind the three little ones for me, the two older ones were at school and I hoped I'd be home in time for when they got out. I had to go to the family courts in Milton Keynes; I had no idea where I was going once I stepped off the train. I didn't have the money for a taxi or bus so walking it had to be. Once out of the station I asked someone the way and all they did was point and say, "It's half a mile up that road." Time was pressing on I had to get a spurt on. I just made it with a little time to spare to have a chat with my solicitor. It was then he told me Keith was applying for custody of Naomi.

I sat in the court while his solicitor came out with the biggest load of crock I'd ever heard.

I was absolutely gob smacked; he told his brief that he did everything for his children he claimed Keith did all the housework, cooking and cleaning because I was lazy and all I did was watch television all day. He also told him about the N.S.P.C.C from years back and made it out in a way that their visit was recent. His solicitor set the tone and now it was Keith's turn to lie under oath. The judge asked him if that was the case then why he didn't take the children with him? He said" I didn't have the room," and then he was asked, "Why was it just Naomi". *The judge loved his reply to this one,* Keith told the court that two of his kids weren't biologically his and the other two were mistakes, "So why should I look after them? they're not my responsibility." The judge then asked him how he thought I was an unfit mother and then say the kids weren't his responsibility. My solicitor then questioned him about when the N.S.P.C.C turned up and what they came out for. It was then Keith started to tell the truth. It was back in 1985 or 86, I'm not quite sure exactly when, and somebody reported Tina. But the allegations were found to be false." It was now my turn to take the stand. The judge had heard enough so I didn't need to give my evidence. He turned to Keith and told him he was a coward and he had no rights to falsify a statement to try to get custody of one child and try to make the mother out to be unfit, custody denied. His solicitor asked for joint custody but again denied full custody was granted to me. He was granted access to all the children once a week and had to pay maintenance on all five children. His solicitor wanted to know if he could appeal against his decision and the judge told him he could try but it would be pointless because no judge would overturn his decision once the transcript of the proceedings had been read. Also, if it was up to him he would grant the decree absolute but even he had to follow the law. All he could do was to grant the decree nisi, and if we got back together within six weeks *(no bloody chance)* then the decree nisi would be cancelled. I couldn't wait for the six weeks to come round to get the decree absolute.

CHAPTER 11
THE BIG C

After the divorce I spent the next few years on my own with my kids. I stopped Keith from visiting them because he was being very unfair, taking Naomi out and spending more money on her and very little on the other two. They were really upset about him not coming around but soon got used to the idea. To add to the stress of it all the council had now decided to re- modernise the house. I had to move to another property in the town. I had the option to move back once the modernisation was completed but this house in the town was ideal. It was just around the corner from the school, which was handy for the kids to walk to and a five minute walk into town. I couldn't have been given a better location and the house was nice too, at least the bathroom was upstairs and not through the kitchen like the other house.

It was now 1988 and I thought things were changing for the better. With the divorce, Keith being the fool he was and the move I was now really unsettled and things started to play on my mind, things from the past the things I tried to forget. They were like a wave washing over me and the demons came back like a bat out of hell, *would I ever be free of them?*

The nightmares and flashbacks, came back with a vengeance *would I ever feel normal and be at peace?* I had to try to get over the Christmas period, a time where families were supposed to be together enjoying the festivities and the coming of the new year. What was there for me to celebrate? I had to make sure the kids had a good time, but I hardly saw any of my family. I felt as though I never existed, I should have been used to it but do you ever get used to it. Would things be different if they knew the truth, maybe? If they did know the truth would it be out of pity? That was something I didn't want was to have them pity me. I couldn't keep on going like this so I eventually went to the doctors and asked for a referral to see a councillor. He asked me why I thought I needed to see a councillor. All I could say was something happened in my past and I needed someone to talk to. The doctor gave me a number to ring and told me that they would help me, it was a local group for people who had suffered as children. That's not what I wanted to do, talk in a group; I didn't know if I could trust them, I didn't know if they were bound to keep things confidential but I did know that a councillor was. They gave me a number for one that had been recommended to them so I made my first appointment for the following week and hoped I wouldn't change my mind by then. I knew I needed help, I just couldn't cope anymore on my own. On the day of my appointment I arrived with a few minutes to spare and all of a sudden; I got an overwhelming feeling that I shouldn't be there. Something didn't feel right, maybe it was nerves? I tried to relax but that wasn't working. Then I was called. On the way to the consulting room, I had a sudden urge to run but by this time I was knocking to go in. When I walked in there was a man sat at his desk reading some paper work. He gestured to me with his hand to sit down, what a rude man not looking up and not a good start to gain someone's trust, *well not mine anyway.* I thought. I sat there for what seemed like an eternity *it was probably a few minutes.* When he eventually looked up you, could have knocked me down with a feather! It was Lew, or rather the spitting image of him. All I could see was the man who took away my childhood and made me suffer all those years ago. I couldn't speak to him, how could I? I looked out of the window all the time I was in there, because in my mind I would have been talking to my abuser. At the end of the session I quickly left his room and as I was passing the receptionist she wanted to know if I'd like to make another appointment. I looked at her and said" Make another appointment? If I ever see this place again it will be too soon." Then, I left and never went back there. I had to do it myself so I put all my energy into making Christmas fun for the kids just as I've always done., It didn't matter how I was feeling, all that mattered was my kids.

Before I knew it, 1990 was looking at me in the face. The year had passed so quickly and I seemed to have missed it. Lack of sleep and trying to cope with five kids had taken its toll on me. The youngest one had now started school so I thought maybe I'd get a bit of time for myself? I'd just finished tidying up and sat down for a few minutes when I was woken by a knock at the door. I must have dozed off. When I answered it, Ann was stood there what a surprise! I hadn't seen her for a few years she asked how me and the kids were I told her we were all fine. I think she knew that wasn't the case just by the look on her face. It must have been the way I said it, she wanted to know if we were doing anything for the half term holidays. I never seemed to plan anything; it was the same every year the kids playing at home with each other or with their friends. She asked me if we would like to go and spend a week with her for a change. Of course, without hesitation, I said "Yes." However, there were still a few more weeks before the kids broke up. I didn't say anything to them in case something changed so they wouldn't get upset; they'd had enough upsets and enough disappointments with Keith so I wasn't going to let them have any more if I could help it.

As the school break was getting closer, I began to wonder why after all this time I was invited to stay and what was Ann up to? Then, I started to wonder should we go? I then thought of the kids. They needed a break away from here for a while and they could see some of the family while we were there. I got busy getting together what we needed for the week then I remembered *silly me* I had no way of getting there. So I rang Ann to see if she could help but she didn't drive. I'd have no choice but to ring Mum to see if they could help me.

Then Ann told me she'd have to ask Henry and ring me back. I was waiting and waiting but Ann never rang back. It was late when the phone rang *about time she got back to me she left it long enough* but when I answered the phone it was Mum, she told me, "Ann had rung and told me that she'd ring you back. I told her that I would do it but forgot and only just remembered." Mum wanted to talk to the kids but they were in bed. Then she told me Henry would pick us up on Saturday. The next day I told the kids. It was a long time since I saw them that excited, they were having a holiday at their aunties! Saturday was here and we were all up bright and early. I was checking I hadn't forgotten anything and the kids were making *sure* that they had their favourite bed toys. Henry arrived just as we finished checking everything. We had a cuppa and a bit of a chat before we set off; even he found it strange that Ann had invited me down, she'd never done it before so why now? We packed everything into the car and set off. It would take about an hour but it seemed like forever to the kids *bless them*. They couldn't wait to see everyone after such a long time. Mum was there waiting with Ann and as soon as the kids saw their cousins the started playing with them. While we sat chatting, a strange, foreign looking man came in. He didn't notice me sat there and started talking to them. Mum realised he hadn't seen me and introduced me to him, "This is Ahamed." Apparently he was from Egypt. I had no idea that Ann was married to him! I felt quite hurt that no one had told me and bloody furious I wasn't invited to the wedding. They'd been married for just over a year and in that time nobody thought to mention it to me. I spoke to Mum once a week and even she didn't say anything *why the secrecy ?* I didn't say anything to them in case it caused an argument. I'd had enough rows in the past so I thought it pointless saying anything. Mum and Dad left, leaving the three of us to chat and the kids were so busy playing they didn't notice them leave. I started to feel uneasy and didn't know why. It was just like all the other times I felt like this but I still couldn't figure it out. The following day was much the same; we sat and chatted and I was getting to know Ahamed a little better. Ann had already told him a little about me but even though we were sisters we didn't really know much about each other *how sad*. The past had done a lot of damage between my brothers and sisters, maybe things will change now? Only time would tell.

A few days later I found Ahamed in the kitchen cooking. He'd cooked so much food *I thought he was feeding an army*. Ann had forgotten to tell me that they had some of Ahamed's friends coming to stay for the weekend, I only found out when three of them turned up on the doorstep. There was Amar and Mustafa. They were married but left their wives at home and then there was Omar he was single. I started to think did Ann forget to tell me? Was she trying to get me hooked up with Omar or was it just me being paranoid? I kept my thoughts to myself. They all seemed friendly enough but, as the saying goes, *never judge a book by its cover*. Over the weekend we all enjoyed ourselves, even the kids had a good time and got on with them all. The weekend flew by and it was time for Ahamed's friends to leave. After they had left Ann asked me, "What did you think of them?" I said, "They seemed nice enough and the kids liked them." She laughed at me and said, "What do you think of Omar?""Which one was that?" Ann was just about to say something when Ahamed walked in so I never got to find out what she was about to say. I assumed she was going to ask me all sorts of questions about Omar. I wasn't ready for another relationship and I was still trying to find what I was looking for. I had a feeling of emptiness and didn't know what was causing it; something was missing and I needed to work out what it was before I could move on. I thought that it could have been someone missing in my life, I suppose that's why I married Keith, *look how far that got me*. I was still on my own or was Keith the wrong one? I didn't know if I was coming or going, my head was all over the place. But, for the first time in a while, I was relatively happy laughing and joking with Ann over silly little things just as we did when we were kids. Mum and Dad came round a few times. I'd not seen them for so long apart from when we arrived. We spent time catching up and before I knew it, the week had almost disappeared. There were just two days left then it was time to go back. The kids wanted to stay longer but schooling had to come first. Amar, Omar, Mustafa and his wife Linda turned up; as soon as Omar saw me be he came straight over and asked me how I was and if I'd had a good week. Why was he being so nice to me? He didn't know me; I became suspicious of him I tried to avoid him for the rest of the time I had there but it wasn't easy. He was a tall, dark, handsome man but as far as I was concerned he wasn't any different from the rest of the men I knew only out for one thing. I'd fallen into that trap before but not this time. Sunday was here and Dad came to take us back home, back to my normality. We said our goodbyes, I told Ann I'd ring her later and off we went. Dad had a quick cuppa before he set off home. Then, I got the younger kids ready for bed and started on getting their clothes ready for school. I lost all track of time and forgot to ring Ann and by now it was too late. I didn't want to chance it in case she was in bed. After taking the kids to school I was having a brew when the phone rang, *bloody hell I'd forgotten Ann again.* I thought it was her wanting to know why I hadn't rang her? When I answered it there was a man's voice at the other end asking he if could speak to Tina, "Speaking," I replied. "It's Omar" said the voice. I wanted to know how the hell he got my number, "Off Ann's mobile phone when she was out of the room, she wouldn't give it to me." I told him he should have got Ann to ring me to see if it was okay for her to give you my number and that he had no right just taking it off her phone without her knowledge. "Would you have said yes," he asked, "We'll never find out know will we now? What can I do for you anyway?" "I'd like to see you again," he replied I told him I didn't trust men but all he wanted was friendship and he didn't have many friends there. I thought here we go, pulling at the heart strings hoping I'd feel sorry for him. In a way I did but I wasn't going to give into him until I made up my mind he genuinely wanted to be just friends or if he had another motive. I couldn't go through life with what ifs and buts so if it was friendship he wanted then I'd be okay with that. The next time he rang me I told him that I wasn't looking for a relationship but friendship would be fine. I gave him my address thinking it would be quite a while before he visited me as he lived in Middlesex and it was quite a way to commute. You could have slapped me in the face with a soggy chip when three days later he was knocking at my door! Katie came in from playing and told me Aunty Ann's friend was at the door. I didn't believe her until I looked out of the window and saw him standing there. I looked around the living room: it was a mess. The kid's toys were scattered all over the place then I remembered Mum always saying, "If friends don't like the way your house is then they know where the door is." Over time things started to develop between us. We were getting closer, a bit closer than I wanted to but we couldn't help it. He proved to be an honourable man. He didn't believe in sleeping with a woman unless they were married. Blow me down with a feather three months later out of the blue he asked me to marry him and I said, "Yes." But, he needed my parents' permission despite the fact I was an adult. In a way I found it rather romantic. The following day we went round to see Mum and Henry. We'd only just got our bums on a seat when he just came it out with, "With your permission, I would like to take your daughters hand in marriage." mum said "Yes." He was waiting on Henry's reply. He tried to explain to Omar that he wasn't my biological father and it wasn't his place to give his permission. Then Omar said to Henry, "You married this woman and took on her children as your own, it didn't matter how old they were." Henry said, "Yes I did." Then Omar said, "In the eyes of the law, that makes you their father, especially with the real father not on the scene." Henry knew what Omar said was right and agreed to him marrying me. The date was set for October, another registry office wedding and this time I would make sure it would be better than the last one. Ann had a big garden so she said the reception could be there she also said we could put up a gazebo and her doing the food wouldn't be a problem. I couldn't afford a new dress but as it happened, one of my neighbours had an off the shoulder lace dress in ivory. It was so beautiful I had to buy it off her. Chantelle and one of her school friends were the flower girls and the weather was amazing for the time of year. All in all it was a beautiful, perfect day. Omar omitted to tell one thing before we married, he would only see me two days a week because of his job. He worked nights in a pizza place making pizzas just outside of London near to his home so it would have be too exhausting for him to commute, especially in the early hours of the mornings and then back again late evening. He got a place nearer to his work but that wasn't much use to me, he still came down to me at weekends. I had a sudden thought! Would he try to change me by getting me to act more like a Muslim woman or would he let me be myself? It actually worked out well him being away all week. I was left to my own devises. This marriage was working out better than I thought it would.

The end of 1991, things changed when I went to have smear test. It was one of those things I had when I felt like it but this time something told me go for it. Good job I did. They found abnormal cells and recommended laser treatment which didn't work. I was then given the option to try the laser treatment again or have an hysterectomy. The decision was an easy one. Omar didn't want kids and I'd already been sterilised back in 1986, five kids were enough so a hysterectomy it was but I had to wait until the April for the operation. I told Omar the situation and he told me not to worry, he'd be there for me and then handed me an envelope. When I opened it inside were tickets and my passport I looked at him and wondered how he got the photos then it dawned on me he asked me to get some photos done so he could put one in his wallet *how sweet of him*. When I looked at the tickets again *oh my God*, I was going to Egypt for two weeks! He'd made all the arrangements with Ann and Marie to have the kids *bless him*. Then I started thinking was there something he hadn't told me, did he have someone else? All sorts of things were racing around in my head, however, I was looking forward to the break and it'd be my first time out of the country so I'd worry about everything else when I got back home. We were leaving from Gatwick so I had to travel down to where he lived during the week. When I arrived at his place, his friends who also lived there with him told me that Omar had gone ahead the previous day and they would make sure I got on the plane on time. He would meet my plane at the other end. I wasn't keen on the idea of flying on my own, especially with it being my first time but he didn't leave me a choice. My nerves were starting to get hold of me as I started to board the plane. I was beginning to wonder if this was a good idea but it wasn't long before the plane was taxiing along the runway and I was in flight.

When I disembarked, I had no idea what to do next. I stood at the carousel and watched all the suitcases go around and around I was dizzy watching them. I eventually got my case and the next thing I knew a police officer came up to me *bloody hell, what have I done?* It was Omar's brother in law. He sent him to meet me. He took me straight past customs to his car; good job he did because Omar's friends only packed some goods that were illegal in Egypt into my suitcase! There was electrical goods and coffee. I was livid when I unpacked my case and found them in there. I couldn't say anything because it wasn't my home and I was the guest but I would have my say when I got back.

I had a fantastic time. I was treated like a queen. Omar arranged a tour guide for me he showed me all the tourist attractions and also the real Egypt where the tourists didn't go. The guide took me to a carpet factory and I was disgusted to see the workforce were children from the poorer areas. For eight hours sometimes more they would work and only got paid one Egyptian pound a day. I was almost in tears and there was nothing I could do. It was the only way their families could eat day by day and it made me realise how lucky we were and how our children had a far better life and future than those poor souls did. Even Omar's nieces and nephews futures were bright. They had an education which was more than those children would ever have. The rest of my holiday was spent thinking about those poor kids working their fingers to the bone for a pittance. I couldn't imagine my kids, or any other kids, doing what they were. Thank god our country doesn't have child labour like they had. I couldn't wait to get home, to see mine and give them the biggest cuddle they'd ever had.

I was back home when reality hit me. I'd left Ann enough money to buy food for the kids while I was away but by the time Marie took over, Ann had spent all the shopping money on takeaways and whatever she wanted instead of buying proper food and cooking for them. As it happened, Marie had some money so she did the shopping and cooked for them. When I found out I asked Ann why. All she could do was keep shrugging her shoulders *it became obvious I couldn't trust my own sister*. I then remembered the operation I was waiting to go in hospital for. The doctor said it was "nothing to worry about" *bloody easy for him to say*. Life went to some sort of normality for the next two and a half months. I made arrangements for the family to have the kids *not Ann.*, The day finally arrived and Alex came to have the kids while Omar took me in. While I was having the pre op he went to make a phone call. After the operation the doctor told me the abnormal cells had turned cancerous in one of my tubes so they had to take away the womb, cervix and the tube. They had got it all but if it returned it would probably be in my breasts so I had to check regularly for any lumps and anything that didn't look right. Then it hit me like a ton of hot bricks. If I hadn't have gone for the test when I did they may never have found it! Or if they had, it would have been to late and they wouldn't have been able to treat it. Then I thought about the kids; what would happen to them? Could I rely on my family or would they put them into care? I was about to let my family now then I changed my mind; what difference would it make? They hadn't really been any support tome in the past so why should it be any different know? They weren't even there when I was going through my divorce with Keith. I started to wonder how many woman don't go for smear tests and end up with cancer, losing their lives because they couldn't be bothered to go just like me. I was lucky that I decided to go this time but I might not have been. I was also wondering where the hell Omar was. I thought he'd be waiting for me after I'd come back from the theatre? Two days later, Omar showed his face *that must have been one hell of a phone call*. I said, "Where have you been?" all he could say was, "I don't like hospitals." He stayed an hour *wasn't I the lucky one?* I arranged for Dad to take me home as I couldn't rely on Omar. He couldn't even give me a proper explanation to where he'd been for two days and I knew Dad wouldn't let me down. When I got home, Alex was still there. I asked him, "Where's Omar?" He told me that he'd not been seen for a week. I was bloody furious! Alex *bless him* took two weeks holiday from work so that he could help me; something my good for nothing husband should have been doing. A week later, I rang Omar to find out when he was coming home only to find out that he'd gone back to Egypt because his family needed him. I was his bloody family and I needed him! I rang Egypt and asked him, "What the hell are you playing at?" I also reminded him of his words to me: "I am going to be there for you." *Like hell he was.* I now knew that the marriage was doomed. We continued for another two years until one day I rang him to tell him not to come that weekend because the kids had colds. Because he worked with food, if he caught it he'd have to take time off.

All he said was "If that's the case I won't be back again." I said to him, "if that's how you feel then I'll have my keys back." That was the end of my marriage to Omar.

CHAPTER 12
THE TRUTH CAME OUT

It didn't take too long for things to get back to some sort of normality yet again but I kept thinking what the hell is wrong with me? Why does this keep happening? I don't deserve it. I sure as hell wouldn't be getting into anymore relationships, not for a long while. Whatever it was I was looking for certainly wasn't marriage. I still didn't know what it was I was looking for, *maybe I'd never find it* but there was still emptiness, a void I couldn't seem to fulfil. Chantelle by now had moved in with her boyfriend Martin. Raymond decided to back pack around the U.K, Naomi moved in with her friends and the other two had their own friends. I was on my own again. Even though I had the two at home, they were busy doing the teenager thing and I still had trust issues. I found it difficult to have a social life but I found a job as a taxi controller. This job helped me to interact with people, something I hadn't done in a lot of years. I eventually became friends with the drivers and became one of the boys, so to speak. They'd ask me to their local boozer after work and occasionally I would go for a pint with them. We'd laugh and joke and I'd enjoy myself for a couple of hours. Sometimes

I'd get asked out but I would tell them where to go and that I wasn't interested; been there, done it, got the T shirt. My circle of friends was expanding and, when I when I could afford it, we'd meet up at the weekend for a drink. Some of them would pop round in the week for a chat and a cuppa which made the loneliness more bearable.

One day Mum had rung me. It was one of her regular calls to see how I was doing and just to have a chit chat but, during the conversation, she let it slip that Lew was in hospital. My voice started to waiver slightly; just the mention of his name sent shivers down my spine and brought back all the memories of what he did to me as a twelve year old child; the memories I tried so hard to suppress over the years. They all knew what I felt about him but they all thought it was because of what he did to Mum, *if only they knew the real reason.* Some of my family said it was all in the past and I should let it stay there, so let sleeping dogs lie and stop letting it eat away at me. At the end of the day he was still our father. Would they still say that if they knew the truth I wondered? The demons inside me were so strong that at night I woke up with sweat pouring off me. I was convinced he was stood at the side of my bed, gloating, I laid there to scared to turn, the sense of him sitting at the end of my bed was so strong. I eventually picked the courage to look, but there was no one there it was just a figment of my imagination. The next day I thought about the night's events. How much more could I take before I had a breakdown. Maybe it was time to tell Mum how Lew ruined my childhood, and maybe my demons would disappear? The only person I could and should tell was my Mum but how much should I tell her? Do I tell her all the sordid details? I kept thinking of excuses for not telling her but all I was doing was driving myself crazy. I eventually picked up the courage and rang her. I said to her "Mum, I need to talk to you but I can't do it over the phone."

She said, "Come over." When I got there, I just looked at Mum and Dad and it just felt as though time stood still. We just stood looking at each other and, like always, the look in Mums eyes told me she knew it was bad news. She could see the pain and despair in mine, then all of a sudden, Marie walked in. I couldn't say anything, the moment had gone. Mum told her to come back later because there was something she needed to sort out with me. Dad went to make a drink and he heard me say that I didn't know where to start. He came in and said, "Try the beginning," then he went back to finish making the drinks. "Before I begin I need to know if there was anything you haven't told Dad about your past," she looked confused and told me he knew everything, I waited for Dad to come back into the room before I started. "Do you remember back in1972 when Lew brought us to see you in prison? and you asked if everything was fine? I think you knew it wasn't. Lew wouldn't leave us alone with you, he was just doing that to prevent me from telling you the truth. The truth being he was not only physically and mentally abusing me he was sexually abusing me as well." "How was he doing this to you?" Mum asked. "At first he just touched me where he shouldn't. Then he went on to raping me and also sodomising me." The look on Mums face, she either didn't understand what I was saying, she was naïve in matters of this nature or she couldn't believe what she was hearing. I had to turn away for a moment to compose myself, when I turned back I could see the tears in her eyes, I wanted to stop but I knew I had to continue. " He told me that if I said anything no one would believe me and that I'd be put into care and he'd tell you that I'd started it." By this time Mum was in floods of tears and I could see Dad was retching, he ran from the room to be sick. When he came back he was pure white. I'd said enough but Mum wanted to know if there was anything else. I didn't know whether to say any more but she told me she needed to know. I carried on, "He told me that if I didn't do what he wanted, he'd ground me so that there was only the two of us and he'd force me. But it didn't stop. He started doing it while everybody was at home. He'd make excuses to get me upstairs to the bathroom where he would make me bend over the bath or toilet. That's when he started anal sex with me and he'd put his hand over my mouth so I wouldn't scream in pain." By now Mum was crying uncontrollably and Dad had to leave the room again he couldn't listen to anymore. She wanted to know how long it went on for, "Until the day I jumped out of the bedroom window for help." I told her Mum became hysterical. All these years I had it in my mind that she knew what was going on but she didn't. She then wanted to know if it I was the only one, what could I tell her? "I don't know, you would have to ask them." I told her. Dad then called me into the garden and asked me "Why did you have to tell her everything?" I told him it wasn't everything but I thought she's heard enough and couldn't take anymore. He then wanted to know what else there was. I told him It didn't matter now. I was thirty seven years old and had been carrying this burden for twenty five years. As for the rest of it I'll probably take that to my grave." He asked no more questions and we went back inside. By the time we got back indoors Mum had composed herself and then asked me, "Is there anything else you want to tell me?" I told her no. I sat there for quite a while, waiting for her to tell me I was lying. She didn't. All she could do was stare out of the window in a daze *hardly surprising*. Dad thought it best if I went home. I didn't want to leave her like that but he said. "I'll take care of her" so I left. All that was going through my mind now was did she believe me? She hated me and wouldn't want to see me again but it was a chance I had to take. I couldn't carry it around with me anymore. I couldn't get on with my life until

I off- loaded the burden and I'd done that now. Three days later, Mum phoned me to see if I was alright. It really should have been me phoning and asking her. Before I got the chance to ask her how she was, she told me that she'd gone to the police to see if anything could be done after so long. According to Mum the police told her there was nothing they could do because it had been too long. I don't know if that was true or not and wondered if was mum trying to protect me from facing him at a trail. I thanked her for trying; now I knew she believed me and didn't hate me or blame me.

There was one question she asked me, "Why did you leave it so long before telling me?" All I could say was, "I didn't think you'd believe me." Things were a bit strained between us for a while afterwards, maybe because she knew there was nothing she could do and she felt guilty, it wasn't her fault, how could she know the man she married in Scotland all those years ago was a paedophile? A few days later, I went to see her. I had to sort things out. I couldn't let her torment herself for the rest of her life, my torment was enough for the both of us. She must have asked the rest of the family if anything had happened to them. Marie and Ann refused to speak to me and I didn't understand why. Mum invited me to a family B.B.Q and, when I arrived, everything stopped. Marie came over to me and, in front of everyone asked me "Why are you lying?" At first I had no idea what the hell she was going on about it was only when Mum came over and told her that this wasn't the time or place I realised what she meant. I asked her, "How could you say that when you didn't know the full story?" She told me she did know the full story because she went to see Lew and asked him. The bastard had told her that it was my fault, that I came on to him and touched him where I wasn't supposed to. That's what he told me he would say all those years ago to stop me from telling. I asked Marie "Are you sure that's what he said" Considering

I was only twelve and knew nothing about sex!" Then she went on to say "You're accusing him because you have to be the centre of attention and I've had enough of you making up stories. If you don't tell the truth, I will never speak to you again." I told her that, "I have no intension of saying anything different because it would be a lie and if we never speak again so be it." Then I walked away. Ann couldn't believe I was willing to upset the family, I wasn't sure if it was all the family or just them. I thought it best that I leave so I said my goodbyes to Mum and Dad and said, "There is no way I can stay with the family thinking I was a liar." Mum tried to persuade me to stay but I couldn't. My was my mind was made up. I got Katie and Alex and gave them the option to stay or come with me. They wanted to come with me, as they saw I was so upset. They asked me if I was alright so I just told them I was fine and there was nothing for them to worry about. I hadn't been home long before the phone rang. It was Mum wanting to know if I was okay and telling me that she would sort Marie out. I told her not to bother because I didn't want them saying that you had picked sides. It was between me and her and anyone else who thought I was lying. I now knew that I was on my own again, *silly me for thinking I could rely on my family to support me.* We had become a family divided. Mum was getting concerned about the way things were going between us all and how divided we all had become so she decided to throw another B.B.Q to see if things could be sorted out. By now they had found out Lew was dying. Mum didn't think it would be such a good idea to tell me, but the rest of them thought I had the right to know. On the day of the B.B.Q Mum had told everyone not to say anything to me and to leave it to her to tell me when the time was right *I don't think mum was going to tell me.* When I arrived, everything was in full swing. The burgers and sausages spitting away on the B.B.Q when all of a sudden Marie shouted over to me, "Dad is dying of cancer! I looked at Mum and asked her, "Where's Henry?" *He's my dad."* It took me a few moments to realise it wasn't Henry, it was Lew she was on about. I glanced at Mum with a disbelieving look and she said "it's true." A little while later I asked Mum which hospital he was in. She told me that it was the local one I then said "I have something I need to do, I'll be back shortly." She knew where I was going but had no idea why. When I got there, I went on to the ward it and walked straight passed him, I didn't recognise him. It wasn't until he called my name I knew which one of the patients he was. As I was walking across to him, there was a nurse there making sure he was comfortable. I stood at the end of the bed and he told me to sit down. I told him it was pointless because I wasn't staying, "I just need to know why you did what you did to me all those years ago? And, to make sure you were dying." The look on the nurse's face was one of shock and horror. He said to me "I didn't do anything." Even on his death bed he was still denying it. As I was walking away, I turned to him and said, "You've never been a father and I'm glad you're dying." *He was getting his just desserts.* The nurse came after me and asked me if that was called for and told me that I should have more sympathy for him. I looked at her and then said, "It has nothing to do with you keep your nose out. If you knew his history then you wouldn't be saying anything. It's your job to look after the patients, not to interfere with family business." I then walked out and never returned. The B.B.Q was still in full swing when I got back to Mum's as if nothing had happened. She asked me if I was okay and I told her that I couldn't be better. Marie wanted to know where I'd been but I wasn't going to tell her the truth so I said, "An old friends," the rest of the day went on without any trouble. Mum and Dad were concerned about me after my visit to them and wondered how I would cope.

It was a pity that they never really knew me and what I was capable of dealing with. The girl that ran away wasn't the girl that came back and Mum couldn't see that.

Marie rang me to tell me that Lew had passed away. She'd let me know when the funeral was and had the audacity to ask me if I would give something towards the cost of it because everyone was putting something in. I politely told her where to go and told her not to ask again. She said she would let me know when the funeral was just in case I decided to go. The day of the funeral came around. I'd made my mind up to go for one reason and one reason only to make sure he was dead and well and truly buried. Everyone was crying, but I just stood there as if I was lost in time. As I saw the coffin being lowered into the ground, I suddenly realised there would be **No Justice**. Marie came over to me and asked me, "Why aren't you upset that he's gone?" "Why should I be upset? I replied, I only came to make sure he had gone and is never going to come back." As I passed the coffin, I spat on it. Some of the family thought I was cold. Maybe I was but I wasn't the one who took my childhood away. Marie said to me "although I don't believe you but, if he did what you said he did to you, couldn't you have forgiven him after all these years?" How can you forgive an abuser someone who broke your spirit and made you into something you're not? It wasn't enough my own father made me feel dirty and worthless not only that he made me a victim now my family are doing that by calling me a liar and saying that I was doing it for attention and they also put Mum in a position of picking sides why should she?, I wasn't going to retract the truth so they could feel better about their father.

Twenty five years of being a victim, the truth came out and I was a victim no more, it's true what they say "what doesn't kill you makes you stronger." And as the song goes. Once I was afraid I was petrified, I will survive and I did survive.

Made in the USA
Middletown, DE
16 April 2018